A runner among falling leaves

A runner among falling leaves

Ciaran O'Driscoll

Liverpool University Press

First published 2001

Liverpool University Press
4 Cambridge Street
Liverpool, L69 7ZU

Copyright © 2001 Ciaran O'Driscoll

The right of Ciaran O'Driscoll to be identified as the author
of this work has been asserted by him in accordance with
the Copyright, Design and Patents Act, 1988.

All rights reserved. No part of this book may be reproduced
in any form without permission in writing from the publishers,
except by a reviewer in connection with a review for inclusion
in a magazine or newspaper.

British Library Cataloguing-in-Publication Data
A British Library CIP Record is available.
ISBN 0-85323-947-9

Set in ITC Giovanni by
Koinonia, Manchester
Printed in the European Union by
Bell and Bain Ltd, Glasgow

First cuts are deepest

PROVERB

Contents

Acknowledgments

With thanks to my wife, Margaret Farrelly, and to Jonathan Williams, for their encouragement and support.

The extract from '1st September 1939' by W. H. Auden on page 171 is reproduced by permission of Faber and Faber and the estate of W. H. Auden; three verses from 'The Isle of Inisfree' by Richard Farrelly between pages 128 and 130 © 1950 Peter Maurice Music Ltd, London WC2H 0QY, reproduced by permission.

1

Defining moments

There is a photograph of me
at about the age of eight or nine in a Hopalong Cassidy suit
sent by cousins in America, a shot taken by my father the
photographer (of 'The Quality Studios', Main Street). In it,
I am radiantly smiling, showing my big new teeth: a boy
who has been rendered beautiful by something his father
said to him which had, for once, struck the right note.
Usually in childhood photographs, I look pensive, distant.

The man who had the power to transform me into a
radiant smiling child rarely exercised this power. And why
so rarely, when it is so easy to make a child smile? What
reservations did he have about me, what rententiveness did
he nurture to the point of rejection? *Don't ever raise your
voice to me again. You're here to cause me a damned sight of
trouble like the rest of them.* So said my father the Master, in
the classroom, publicly, in front of the assembly of third-
to sixth-class children, in the rural two-teacher school
where he was principal, big fish in a small pond, with such
a capacity to inflict damage.

Words I never forgot. And what did I feel the day they were spoken? That was a day in autumn when leaves were showering from the trees, and at breaktime the children ran wildly ecstatic in the wind, clutching at leaves as they ran, and I ran with them not to be different; something told me 'Run with the others, hide this misery of an unwanted child, this desolate grief that cannot express itself or shed itself in tears. There is no one to turn to: run, run and shout and gesticulate, mimic that wild abandon, clutch like the others at falling leaves.' My father, in one of his long-lasting moods, stood at the school door, watching, not seeing.

Under the rubric of lessons in General Knowledge or Christian Doctrine (in those days, it was hard to tell one from the other) my father shared his apocalyptic fears with his pupils. Wars and disasters, the growth of Communism, speculation about the Third Secret of Fatima, *The Irish Catholic*'s prophecy of Three Dark Days which would descend on earth in 1960, when the powers of darkness were to be loosed on the world.

Stalin was said to be dying, and my father had us praying for Stalin, because (who knew?) Russia might have a more hostile leader after him. I prayed for Stalin's life, but I, too, was dying. I was dying without knowing it. I didn't know a father's love, and didn't know that not having a father's love was a kind of dying. The photograph bears witness to the truth: it is so easy to raise a child from the dead – simply say the right word. You may not feel it at the time; the feeling will come later. Only say the word, it is so simple to say, that can raise a child from the dead. But *you* wouldn't say it, would you? You were too worried about Stalin.

You were too worried, full stop. Whatever it was you needed was somewhere in the future; it was coming, you were waiting for it. And the waiting took up your whole life, so that you had no time for me; I was there only to cause you *a damned sight of trouble*. When things were better for you, then you would be better with me; you knew that. Only for the lack to be filled and everything to be transformed: you waited for that miracle to happen because you couldn't say the kind words I needed beforehand. And time passed by and I grew up and became a man, and you were still frustrated, things didn't change; the only thing that happened was that time sped by and it was too late. I was gone. As simple as that. If only you had realized that a child was a gift from the gods, that I was a miracle...

Ganntanas, easpa, ceal, díth, díobháil, uireasa, gá: you gave us so many Irish words for lack that our heads were addled with them. You pronounced them with fervour, words from our language, accumulated over our history; so many different ways of naming the void. But you also spoke them with a certain relish – perhaps the satisfaction of looking back on harder times from a present when you at least had plenty to eat.

During teacher training, you once told me, you and your friends were so hungry that you raided turnip fields. You were one of the agitators trying to initiate a strike because of the quality of the food in your training college, and believed you were victimized afterwards as a malcontent. You knocked on presbytery doors looking for work in the early days after qualifying, and parish priests slammed them in your face. And when you finally got a job, you were terrified to leave its security and take the risks of your art, especially as our good Catholic uncontracepted family grew, and each one of us proved as hungry as you. And so you lectured us endlessly, bored us to a kind of death about the sacrifices you were making for us.

You were not accepted, a stranger in a small Irish town. Respected, because you were a teacher, but not accepted. It was a kind of death, I know. But you had me if only I had counted as anything to you. I would have accepted you; I could have given you life if you had let me. It's all in that radiance, that image of unfulfilled promise: you were God calling me from the cloud, and my smile replied, *Master, here I am.* But you only wanted my smile to make a good photograph, one that might be published in *The Amateur Photographer,* and when the shutter clicked, the apparition of kindness disappeared and I was banished again into exterior darkness.

Ours is a world dominated by ambition, and ambition sucked you into its vortex, all the more tragically because you were ineffectual, you couldn't handle the velocities in there; ambition sucked you in and spewed you out, dismembered, on failure's beach. You didn't get through in one piece to the other side. And your ineffectual ambition choked off the possibility of one magnificent achievement that would have cost little: to be remembered as a true father, a real father, your memory to be a glow of love and pride in your children's minds. *But what a father we had,* we'd say, whatever might betide us. Now I want to cry for my lost father, but I hold back my tears, because you were more than lost; I never knew you. And I cannot cry for a father I never knew. If I weep, I weep for myself, for never having known a father. And that's as near as I can get.

⤴

First cuts are deepest, they say. It must surely have been the moment of my first cut, when my father spoke those words. Almost half a century after they were spoken, the wound they made still festers. It was a moment when words and vulnerability met to create a terrible illumination: *this is my father, and this is my life.* To this day, I remember the two sentences just as they were uttered, in their exact phrasing and syntactical order. My father's idiomatic peculiarities: the *damned sight of trouble* I was causing him; an awful lot of trouble, perhaps a much-cursed panoramic view of the affliction that having children can bring to those who want to fulfil themselves in other ways. The rhetorical litotes of *Don't ever raise your voice to me again,* which I knew meant *Don't ever speak to me again.* I knew that was what it meant because I hadn't shouted or spoken loudly to him at all, or given him the kind of backchat which, even in a low voice, he would definitely have heard loud and clear, due to the excellence of his hearing which he never tired of boasting about: *I may have bad eyesight but I have very good ears.*

I had provoked him simply by giving the incorrect answer to a question; I forget the details, but I deduce that the question must have come from either arithmetic or Irish grammar, subjects he had been browbeating me about for many weeks prior to and after that defining moment, both literally beating me about the brow for incorrect answers and applying sustained pressure of interrogation as if he could force the correct answers out of my head by those methods: as if the best way of educating children was for a schoolmaster to adopt the techniques of the Special Branch.

My father took extra care with the education of his own children. Education was a war, and we were the spies who were singled out for special treatment. The other children were mere soldiers, and were dealt with in a more detached, perfunctory way: the *bata* on each hand, two or four or six slaps in all, depending on the severity of the transgression, and no more about it; they went back to their desks, crying or not crying, walking brazenly with head erect or crouched in an absurd shuffle, their hands gripped tightly between their knees. But the spies had to be treated differently, and I, as the eldest of his children, was the first spy to enter my father's interrogation room, the room of the higher classes from third to sixth. The method of dealing with spies had to be tougher because they were assumed to have superior knowledge, and the interrogator would be hugely satisfied to hear a spy divulge this critical information in front of the footsoldiers, who would know when they heard it that they were doomed to defeat and a lifetime of slavery. But for some reason I was a dud spy; I just didn't have the crucial data my father wanted me to reveal. I was a spaced-out spy who hadn't concentrated during the vital briefings.

And so my father, the Master, the expert on information extraction, baffled and enraged, beat me up and down the classroom, with repeated handslaps to the head and face, and punches to the shoulders. *How often do I have to ask you? How many times do I have to go over it? You'll listen by the time I'm finished with you. I'll teach you to listen.* He spoke in a cold fury, and often there was spittle on his lips. Then he'd leave off, defeated, breathing heavily, and go back to his raised desk at the top of the classroom, to sit sulking about his miserable life, while the dumbfounded pupils wondered what they should be doing. Once, as I was heading back to my desk, numbed by beating and berating, I caught a furtive look of pity in another boy's eye. That look set me apart.

My parents didn't keep me from children who were rough. But the rough children took pity on me because no one kept me from my father.

Dad, let me tell you something. Now that you're dead, I can speak frankly to you at last, in a way I could never do when you were alive, because no sooner would I begin than you'd get into a huff and go to lie on your bed and an atmosphere would descend on the house and my mother would begin the tea-ceremony: emissaries of peace sent up to you at half-hourly intervals to ask would you like a cup. And maybe the fifth or the sixth or the seventh delegate (we're running out of volunteers, we're on the second round) would come back with an olive branch between his teeth, the joyful message that our father, the Master, will deign to take a cup of tea in a quarter of an hour and after that he wishes to address us all, Mother included, about the sacrifices he has made, is making and must continue to make on our several behalves.

15

At first, Dad, I wanted to write all this from some lunatically objective point of view, as if you were a remote kind of third person and I, even as the first person of the story, was detached from myself, in the manner of looking back on what's past and done with. But who was it said that *the feelings never age?* And why was it that whenever I visited you in your later years, even when you were a decrepit old man and I could have battered you to death (and perhaps I should have), why was it that even then the first emotion I always felt was fear? Springing up out of those ageless childhood days came a fear that you would say some other terrible sentence to add to the first two that I never forgot.

And the truth is I never forgot them because you never retracted them. It was some twisted point of honour with you that you would never apologize for anything. It's commonly accepted now that people of your generation weren't particularly at home with the expression of affection, and never doubted that they had a right to punish children physically, a now-discredited right which they often confused with giving vent to hostility and personal frustration; classic Freudian substitution, like the clerk who comes home and kicks the cat because the boss has given him a hard time at the office.

But I've heard stories from friends about their own childhood beatings, and how their fathers, unable to apologize, were not so singleminded as to be without remorse, and would leave some little present, an orange, a packet of sweets, by the bedsides of the sleeping victims of their anger. But not so you, Dad; you were too *beyond it all* for that. You lived in another world. You were some kind of Hindu god, swiping many-handedly at the child-faced flies that buzzed around your all-hallowed, irascible head.

That day almost half a century ago brought my defining moment, my moment of insight. Not a moment that defined me, but a moment in which I saw and understood my preconceived definition. *You* were what defined me. I was defined by the kind of father I had, and there was no possibility of exchange. Mine was the in-itself sonship that would never be for-itself. When you spoke those words, I began to drown and saw a life unfold before my eyes; but it was your life, not mine. You had imposed yourself on my personality; you were the sea I was drowning in. You told us all about the Fall of Man in your Christian Doctrine lessons, and later, in secondary school, I read that John Henry Newman, before converting to Catholicism, had some kind of intuition of a 'great aboriginal calamity'. That day of your two unforgettable sentences, I had a similar intuition, but less general, less historically sweeping: that you were my very own, my private aboriginal calamity.

⌐

I remember another defining moment from this period of my childhood: my father and Barbara, our housemaid, playfully, flirtatiously hip-butting one another in the kitchen. They are doing this openly, before my eyes and the eyes of my brothers and sister, after dinner. My mother, as usual, is absent. She is out serving customers in our grocer's shop; that was why we needed a housemaid.

17

Barbara was the daughter of a small farmer. I have inherited many photographs of her. There is one which shows her at home on the farm, forking wheat or barley on to the top of a threshing machine. The curves of her plump body – 'pleasingly plump' as they say; well certainly pleasingly so to my father – can be inferred from her raised posture, despite the bagginess of her working overalls. You can see that her neck, though thick, is graceful; her face aslant towards the sky is high-boned, her lips are full. She looks proud of her youth and prowess. You can see the strong clench of her hands on the pitchfork, the strength of her bare arms. Above her head, the corn is separating itself from the prongs of the fork, becoming airborne. It will land on top of the thresher, where a man is waiting to shovel it down into the maelstrom of machinery that separates the grain from the chaff. Those strong hands, those bright arms, were frequently raised to wallop the living daylights out of me.

The memory of that hip-butting incident is a window in which, every now and then, the repressed feelings of my childhood appear suddenly like a dancing ghost. A sad ghost dancing with uncontrollable envy and rage. To think that my father could have liked Barbara more than me, his first-born child, more than my mother, more than the rest of his children. But the sting of the memory is even worse: here were our two bad-tempered beaters – Barbara often took up where my father left off – in an unholy alliance, *having fun with one another*. My father, who never played with us, now playing with his accomplice in our physical abuse. And what kind of game were they enjoying that made me feel so bad?

A *lighting bitch from hell.* That's how I once described Barbara. I was very surprised to hear the words coming out of my mouth at the time they did, because I was a novice in a religious order, speaking to my spiritual director. I think there must have been some deep unspoken hatred between me and Barbara. Did she somehow detect the envy and rage I wasn't able to express, and was that why she beat me so much, at the slightest provocation? Had I been cast in the role of stand-in for my mother in this love triangle, seeing that she was always in the shop? Was my hurt deeper than my mother's, who didn't seem to be aware of what was going on? Perhaps in Barbara's mind I was the real, the substantial rival for my father's affections because under my 'reaction formation' of fearful compliance she could sense the hatred, alive as it is today.

My father once took a photograph of Barbara washing a wooden kitchen chair with scrubbing brush and soap. He must have treasured that smile she gave him, looking up from her curious task: smile of the eyes, of the whole face, not just a mouthful of teeth. Something in that look is meant not only for the camera but also for him. From that small photograph my father cut out a rectangle round Barbara's head and enlarged it into several 8″ × 6″ prints, then replaced the rectangle in the original with sellotape. Seeing Barbara's face more clearly in the larger prints, I am convinced that here is the look that unhinged my father. What was it: love or fancy or promise? A look that says *my hero, my sugar daddy, my deliverer*? Or was it simply a young woman's look of plain liking, which my father blew out of all proportion?

I imagine that those enlargements were mementoes: by the time he made them, the negative of the small print must have been lost; and perhaps Barbara had already left for America.

Relics of a passion; my pyrrhic victory.

⤿

I suffer from anxiety. I have a little black notebook in which I write down ideas, images and memories that might be relevant to this memoir. Occasionally I jot down a dream, as in the following entry:

I dreamt I was arrested for Chronic Anxiety. The policeman said he understood my unfortunate situation and that he might be able to get me off without a summons. He left me in a waiting room. Suddenly I realized I could be there for hours because the place, with all its different alcoves and open-plan rooms, was crowded. Full of anxiety, I began pacing the floor.

There are other details, but the main point for present purposes is that the dream is perhaps punning on the word 'arrest': I (in my development) have been arrested, not *for*, but *by* chronic anxiety.

I connect this idea with a moment of insight described by the psychologist Rollo May in his book *The Courage to Create*. He was doing a thesis on the incidence of anxiety among a group of unmarried mothers who had been banished from home by their parents. His argument was that all these women should show symptoms of anxiety, but to his surprise only half of them did. May was more interested in describing the creative process of insight (whatever the insight), but it is the content rather than the form of his discovery that interests me here: he realized that the women (mainly working-class) who didn't display anxiety were under no illusion that they had been rejected and as a result simply moved on with their lives; they had troubles, but they didn't worry about them. The anxious women were mainly middle-class and were still receiving, and accepting, assurances of love from the parents who had banished them. The roots of their worry were cultural: a matter of holding on to beliefs which contradicted their real situation.

I believe the roots of my own anxiety are analogous. As a child, part of me – the Platonic part – couldn't believe what was happening. Those blows to the head and face, those punches on the shoulder, the rejecting words, had to be dismissed because I was living in the Holiest Country in the World where good Christian parents brought up their children according to the model of the Holy Family at Nazareth. The hidings and harsh judgments were an aberration, a kink in the scheme of reality, some kind of gap through which unreality attacked. But no matter how viciously unreality struck, it didn't make the slightest difference: I still had a Catholic father (the best kind of Christian father) who modelled his actions on the life of St Joseph the Carpenter, and I was living in the country that was dearest to the heart of the Pope in Rome because of its devout adherence to the Faith through centuries of persecution, *in spite of dungeon, fire and sword.* It was impossible that my father would reject me; so how could it be that he *was* rejecting me? But there was another part of me taking stock of what was actually (i.e. 'unreally') happening: and that is the raving ghost which now appears at the window of memory.

The most unfortunate thing is that my father seems to have spent his life in a state of amnesia regarding the havoc he wreaked on us at that period: his bad-tempered assaults did not fit his official image, so he promptly forgot them. The most I could wring from him by way of a concession in later years was that he sometimes administered 'mild chastisement' (which was officially approved by Church and State) for our own good.

The adults in my town walked past me every day and no one knew I was a child who was suffering. It was worse than that: they didn't know that children could suffer. There was no one to approach for help. It was worse than that: the language spoken by adults had no words for what I was going through, for what I might have to endure. Jesus loved the little children. I was in a condition without a name. I took my absence from their thoughts, from their language, for granted, and accordingly absented myself from my own thoughts, from my own language. Even in the confession box I couldn't confess my father's sins; they had to be my own. Can nothing on this sad earth spread its wings and fly?

My father's passion was photography. Looking for the right light, the right facial expression, he sacrificed us on the altar of his art. And on the altar of his frustration, since photography demanded endless time, and didn't provide him with money, and so he had to teach (a permanent pensionable job) in order to feed, clothe, house and educate us. And that meant he didn't have the endless time photography demanded. Therefore his job had to come first (he was very scrupulous about it), but photography was a good second, and we spent eternities posing for him, or under orders not to leave the parked car while he went in search of photographs by lakes and headlands during our summer holidays, accompanied by his secondary passion, the housemaid, the *mott*, the *quare wan*, his photographic muse, the natural companion of the male photographer, the good-looking woman. Well, as good-looking as he could get: Barbara. (Who wasn't all that bad-looking, I have to admit, when I look at the carefully angled shots of her I have inherited.)

Did you butter her up, Dad, with promises of photographic fame, appearances in *The Amateur Photographer* and *Photography*? How different for her it must have been from forking grain into a thresher, to be driven around the Irish coast, to be a model, to pose by lakes and on beaches, to be valued for her appearance alone, rather than her ability to scrub floors, make meals and clip children's ears.

My mother told me recently that one year a Christmas tree haunted our parlour until Easter. My father insisted that it stay there until he got the time and the equipment to take a shot of 'The Wonder of Christmas Night': this photograph is now in my possession, my first brother and my sister staring in fake wonder at fake presents under the unseasonal tree.

The ghost that appears at memory's window is condemnatory, unforgiving; but it has to have its say. It looks at a photograph called *Happy Trio*, and goes into a paroxysm of rage at the sheer falsity of it: the simpering smiles of Hilary and Anthony as they offer daffodils to smiling Barbara, whose arms are around their shoulders. The ghost is quick to point out the way Anthony is leaning slightly back from Barbara, an involuntary piece of body language from a nervous system habituated to recoiling from this arm which is now in an unaccustomed mode of embracing.

It's a lie! It's a lie! rages the ghost. *Tear it up, throw it in the fire. Throw them all in the fire.*

And what of this photograph which shows John Daniel, our youngest at the time, naked in the bathtub, Barbara crouched on the floor beside him, both of them with fists raised in the on-guard position of boxing? And the cringingly sentimental title, *Don't hit her: she's too nice*, written in pencil on the back? Still, there are times when I catch sight of something else, looking through these photographs; times when the ghost is sleeping, and I get a sudden glimpse of my father's inner life, his hopes and dreams, his naivety, the blindness of his infatuation.

24

2

Mother and child schemers

It was my first brother, Anthony, who showed me my father's love-letters to our housemaid. He had rummaged them out of a cardboard box in the attic. I have no idea whether these love-letters were ever actually received; or whether, Victorian-style, they had been received and returned, betokening impossibility or rejection. Perhaps they had never been sent, and were simply my father's way of giving expression to his forbidden feelings.

My therapist, a tall, thin, basketball player of a man, holds me with his glittering eye. He exudes superiority, much as he tries to conceal it under a professional mien. His smugness tells me I am considerably below his level in the matter of figuring out and coping with life and society. Already I nurture strong feelings of hostility towards him which, if I revealed them, he would regard as an indication that the therapy is progressing well: the unconscious 'transference' on to him of my feelings towards my father is well under way. But somehow I know in my heart and soul that I dislike him for himself. I am also convinced that he

25

dislikes me, because I am not compliant enough to his theories. I have told him that I see my life as a simple matter: I will struggle on, and then die. His professional ego, however, will be satisfied only by a transformation, an unleashing of buried potential, a *change in the internal structure* of my personality. If ever I get angry and aggressive in his clinic, it will be with him, not with him-as-my-father.

On the other hand, he has set me an interesting exercise in relation to my father's love-letters: to write about how I felt the day Anthony showed them to me.

I don't know if I had any emotion at the time. Certainly not a very clear one. Perhaps a dull or smothered feeling of disappointment, a sense that my father's rejection of me was once more confirmed. Perhaps I didn't want to believe the evidence or know what to make of it. How could it be that this was the world I was emerging into, a world where fathers were capable of betrayal, where my father was capable of betraying me, where children lived perpetually on the edge of betrayal?

I don't think that the question *Will my father leave us and run away with Barbara?* ever crossed my mind. That question was not allowed; the boundaries of my understanding were narrower than would permit it. It's also probably true that the boundaries of what my father thought possible were similarly narrow, and his sense of constriction, of being trapped, accounted for his anger and frustration. I am referring, after all, to Catholic Ireland of the 1950s, where divorce did not exist and where, officially speaking (in the Holiest Country in the World), there were no extra-marital carryings-on.

26

I know that my therapist will not be happy with the final sentences in the above paragraph. I am veering away from the task of unearthing my anger towards my father, and trying instead to understand his point of view. There is something in me still that wants to protect my father, perhaps because he was *my* father, the only father I ever had.

~

After a few sessions, my therapist announces that my father abused me not only physically and mentally, but also sexually. 'In those auto-erotic fantasies of your teens,' he tells me, 'you were re-enacting what happened between you and your father; you were continuing to try and please your father.'

I wonder how my therapist can be so certain of this, given that I have no memory of sexual abuse. Is he not jumping to conclusions? Should he not wait and let me be the one to make such a discovery? Eventually I have a dream that I am in bed with my father and he is forcing me to hold his penis and bring him to orgasm. But I still have no memory of sexual abuse. The horrible thing is that my therapist may have irresponsibly planted the idea in my mind, and that the dream is a result of suggestion.

On the subject of *Pleasing my father,* I wonder did anyone ever please him in those far-off constricted days? Did Barbara please him in those long photographic sessions by the lakes in West Cork, when they were hidden from view for hours by the reeds, and we children were in the car parked by the roadside, under instructions not to stir from there? Officially my father was waiting for the right light;

he stood for hours with a light meter in his hand, watching the needle, while Barbara sat beside the water reading *Woman's Own*. Eventually, he'd return to the car, complaining about the poor light and the cloud that had interfered at the crucial moment.

Judging from my father's and Barbara's humour when they returned, whatever took place by the lakes was more a matter of frustration than consummation.

↩

My mother was the 'sympathetic other', the nice woman who lived in the shop. She didn't know much about what was happening in the living quarters, the goings-on between my father and Barbara, the frustrated flirtations and the reign of terror.

She was the friendly shopkeeper next door who sometimes came on a visit. Always when she came, one or other of us was crying or had a sorrowful tale to tell, so she became an ambassador from the outside world, a bringer of consolation and the promise of change on the horizon. 'Ah sure, don't mind it, boy. He'll get over it. Things won't always be like this.'

When she tried to play mother, my mother always got it wrong. I think she had this idea that a mother was someone who kept the peace between a father and his children, a big mistake in our case because it amounted to placating a tyrant. She was the inventor of the lugubrious tea-ceremony already described. That particular ritual of placation lasted for decades, because even when we came visiting as adults, some childhood fallout with a long half-life would send my easily infected father to the nuclear shelter of his bedroom, from where he would have to be cajoled by the false all-clear of the cup of tea. Then one day, when he left the kitchen because of some remark I had made (I was one hundred and fifty-eight at the time and he had just turned five million and one), one of my brothers asked 'What's wrong with him now?' and suddenly my mother made a pre-emptive strike against her own ritual by announcing with great firmness, 'Leave him be. He'll come out when he's hungry.' And that was the end of the long dynasties of the tea-ceremony.

It was always better for us when my mother came in as the friendly shopkeeper, with that promise from the outside world: *things won't always be like this.* Somehow, she was able to speak words like that with affection and a quiet conviction that reassured us, battered and disconsolate as we might have been. I preferred my friend the shopkeeper to my mother, because my mother shared the same degradation as her children: she was motivated in everything she did by her fear of the tyrant. In a strange way, perhaps, she was more of a mother when she wasn't trying to be one, by coming to us from the outside world with sympathy and a message of hope.

Mothers and children weren't highly regarded in those days. There was a humanitarian government minister who tried to introduce a 'Mother and Child Scheme', and it led to one of the greatest uproars the country has known.

To this day my friend the shopkeeper is still telling me that *things won't always be like this,* and I don't know where

29

she gets the strength to do it. My therapist, however, assures me that I have yet to tackle my anger towards my mother.

↬

I sometimes try to imagine what it would have been like if we children had got together and instituted a campaign of resistance, with the aim of deposing my father from his insufferable patriarchal position. It would hardly have been possible in those days, but what we needed was a *coup de famille*. The next time my father went to lie sulking on his bed, we, the Revolutionary Committee of the Back Yard, could have unanimously agreed to refuse my mother's nervous conciliatory demands.

'Anthony, will you go up and ask him would he like a cup of tea?'

'No I will not, Mammy. I only said that he was more like the school bully than the headmaster. Let him rot up there. Or else let him come down and apologize for making us all so miserable.'

'Well I don't know what's got into you, Anthony. That's a terrible thing to say. Darcy, will you go up? That's the good boy.'

'No, Mammy. None of us are going up to him. And you're not to go up either. He has us all terrorized and our life isn't worth living. Neither is yours.'

'And another thing, Mammy. You'll have to get rid of Barbara. She's as bad as him. And you're a fool if you think it's photographs he's taking when be brings her with him on holidays.'

'No, Mammy. We think he wants to put his gilly in between her legs.'

'Well I declare to God, I don't know what's got into ye all. God help me. What am I going to do with ye?'

'There's nothing has got into us, Mammy. We only want a decent life. And you need one as well. Get rid of Barbara right now, and I'll go and tell him he can stay up there till the roof falls on top of him for all we care. We're taking no more shit from him and that's a fact.'

I wonder what would have happened. Would my father have gone to the guards and the parish priest, would the religious and secular powers, operating in concert, have surrounded the house with sirens wailing and marksmen on neighbouring roofs and thuribles flying and holy water? Would we wake the following morning to find that the front door had been daubed with the legend *Mother and Child Schemers*?

But this is facetious exaggeration and masks the stern reality: judging from some recent television programmes on the period and the nature of the legal-institutional complex of the time, it is quite possible that we would have been sent to an orphanage if my mother had joined the rebellion and my father had stood his ground.

In any case, the probability of reprisals was too high to risk revolt. Instead, my father would eventually be persuaded to come down, and my mother would serve him tea with placatory attention. When he had finished his morose slurping, he'd call us from the back yard and give us a long lecture on the sacrifices he was making for his family, comparing them to the sacrifices made by the great fighters for Irish freedom, the sacrifices of Pearse and MacDonagh, of Wolfe Tone and Robert Emmet, of Kevin Barry and Red Hugh O'Donnell and Brian Boru.

～

Let's play the game of getting Daddy to say a sentence. Because if we manage to get him to say a full sentence, even a short one, there will be less fear and tension in the house. Because one sentence leads to another, and he'll get into the spirit of saying things. He'll get his voice back and start saying very important things and feel in charge again. He won't go up to his room and lie on the bed after silently scraping the last piece of white from the shell of his supper egg. He's done that for three evenings in a row now, and when Mother comes in from the shop, and asks *Where is he?* her face falls when we tell her *He's gone up to lie on the bed.*

Let's play the game of getting Daddy to say a sentence. Ask him what's the capital of Timbuktu. That might even have wrung a smile from him in a different world.

～

While I was writing the first draft of this memoir, my wife came home one evening from a bookfair and handed me a copy of a pamphlet entitled *Punishment in Our Schools*, published in April 1955 by the Schoolchildren's Protection Organization. The pamphlet contained an essay on the prevalence of excessive corporal punishment in many Irish schools, and a set of excerpts from harrowing letters written to the organization by parents and guardians of physically and mentally abused schoolchildren.

Reading the pamphlet was something of a shock to me: I was so preoccupied with the expression of my own experiences as a child that I had lost sight of the general context in which they had occurred. Of course I knew in theory that we weren't the only children who had suffered, but the pamphlet, especially the raw descriptions of abuse in the excerpted letters, brought the general situation home to me with fierce impact: I was one case, not just among five or six, but among thousands.

Here were accounts of children maimed at school, hiding their bruises for fear of greater punishment, huddled up in themselves in fear. Sometimes they couldn't keep their sorrow in: they sobbed in their beds in the middle of the night and their sobbing was overheard. Then they showed the marks on their bodies, the welts on their hands and the backs of their legs, the swollen ears, the dislocated finger-joints, the places where the hair was torn out, the gaps where teeth were missing. They told of being placed sitting on high windowsills, slate boards tied around their necks with the word *Dunce* chalked on them; they told of standing all day in corners of classrooms, not being allowed to eat or go to the toilet. The parents went to teachers and headmasters and were verbally abused. They wrote to the Department of Education and were abused by silence.

Helpless parents have written about how they had to suffer in silence, watching their children suffer and unable to do anything about it. A child beaten because a labouring man couldn't provide her with two pence in mid-week for a supposedly voluntary elocution class; a child ostracised by his teacher for being out of school for a week because of illness. The parents helpless because they have exhausted all recourse and cannot find another school within walking distance. Because they will be served with a summons if they keep their children at home. Because they cannot afford to take the matter to court.

Don't wonder why the world is upside down when it could be no other way. Thus wrote a woman in one of the excerpted letters. She describes herself and her family as 'only labouring people in a cottage'. But in a way she was a philosopher, with an understanding of cause and effect far superior to that of my father and all the others in the social strata above her.

But the children whose mental and physical injuries are described in the pamphlet were perhaps, comparatively speaking, lucky. The fact that a letter was sent to the Schoolchildren's Protection Organization meant that their parents, or some relative or adult friend, sympathized with them. There was an adult in their lives who validated their sense of wrong.

And how does our particular case fit into this general context? In one way, judging from the more harrowing descriptions of physical abuse in *Punishment in Our Schools,* it emerges that we got off (relatively speaking) lightly. But in another way our situation was worse, because the punishment was inflicted by our own father, and often did not stop when school was over. There was no escape from the angry teacher: he drove us home, where he frequently resumed unfinished business from the classroom. In this way our fate was akin to that of abused children whose parents thought that if a teacher beat them, it was deserved, and gave them more for good measure.

If only the Revolutionary Committee of the Back Yard had known of the Schoolchildren's Protection Organization! We could possibly have persuaded our mother to write to them; she could have shown us the reply and the enclosed copy of *Punishment in Our Schools*. And then we would at least have known that we were not alone. We might even have been able to frighten my father by telling him that there was an organization in the country which considered his actions criminal and was working to bring him to justice.

↝

It was worse if you got the *bata* on a cold day than on a warm day. It was twice as worse if it was your turn to start the fire and you couldn't start it, and your father the Master was standing behind you saying *Go on! Are you afraid of it or what?* And you weren't afraid of the match, only afraid that the big bully-boy would hit you across the head if you couldn't light it because your fingers were so cold.

And when at last you were able to light the match and put it to the fire, nothing but smoke came out between the lumps of coal, and then nothing at all, not even smoke. And *How often do I have to tell you how to do it?* said your father the bully-boy Master and gave you the *bata*, twice on each hand.

It was twice as worse and made you want to cry, not only because the pain of frozen hands is more awful than the pain of warm hands, but because you felt ashamed of not being able to light a fire, and you hated those lousers of flames that died down after a few seconds and left nothing but smoke, and then nothing at all only you rubbing your hands to try and rub the pain out of them, until at last the blood came back and they felt better.

There was only one proper way of lighting a fire, said the Master, just as there is only one proper way of doing anything.

A fire had to be built like a crow's nest, with twisted-up bits of paper at the bottom, and over them criss-crossed twigs, and then the crows sitting on top, the black lumps of them. And you set the nest on fire under the crows; you put the match to the twisted bits of paper on the bed of the nest, and the flame was supposed to spread to the twigs that were the sides of the nest, and finally set the shagging crows on fire.

But the twigs were too damp or else they didn't burn for long enough to light the crows, and the crows just sat there, you couldn't smoke them out like ordinary crows, nothing worked except to burn the bastards. They couldn't fly, these lousy kinds of crows, they just fell and rolled around the grate when their nest collapsed. These were the kinds of dirty hoors of crows that got you the *bata* and made the other children grin at one another behind your back, because the Master's son wasn't able to light a fire.

And then, when your father lit the fire himself, he took a photograph of you warming your hands at it, just you crouching down with your hands stretched out above the flames, and nothing else in the photograph only the fireplace with the tongs and bellows on the other side from you. As if it wasn't happening in school at all and your father wasn't the Master who had caned you for not being able to light the fire; as if you were just an ordinary boy who had come home for a while to warm his hands and then ran out to play again until it was time for supper.

And your father called the photograph *It's Cold Outside.* But really it was much colder inside; your father had made everything inside you colder than cold.

↜

My father had made everything inside me colder than cold and part of me was condemned to search, throughout my life, for his absent warmth, the glow of his love and approval. In occasional moments of illumination, this unconscious programme revealed itself. There was, for example, the music-making incident that occurred when I was about thirty-five.

About a year before, I had begun learning the tin whistle and, on a visit to my parents, I was playing some reels or jigs in the kitchen. My father was talking to a neighbour in the next room. I played on and on, slowly becoming aware of a gnawing dissatisfaction. I thought at first that the tunes had grown stale through repetition. But I suddenly realized that there was something all-too-familiar about the scene, which triggered an ageless discontent: my father talking to someone else while I am doing a deed I want him to notice and approve; a man of thirty-five wanting to please his father with music, to be patted on the head and told 'Good boy'.

A sense of futility probably added to that gnawing dissatisfaction: there was another unconscious programme, the contradiction of the first, which would have dismissed any words of praise from a rejected father.

I was a split tin-whistle player: making music both to please my father and to overshadow him.

3

The great sliced pan in the sky

My brother Anthony, that wily lad: he was the one who understood the situation from the start. He didn't live in hope; he was having none of it. To him a spade was a spade, and a charade was a charade. Always light years ahead of me in worldly wisdom, Anthony one day thrust my father's love-poems into my face. *Oh Barbara of the bright breasts*: he showed me this opening line and giggled. *A Bharbara na gcíoch geal.*

Headlights, he informed me, was what they called breasts in the New Houses, and my brother had friends living in that council estate strewn with broken glass. One day he told me, 'You put your gilly in between a woman's legs and the spunk goes into her belly, and after a while a baby comes out.' I thought that *after a while* maybe meant a few minutes. I was appalled: it all seemed so sordid.

Anthony took a few looks at life, and a nod was as good as a wink. OK, he said to himself; this is what it's like and I'm stuck with it. Rather than being a nomad like me, retreating through a shrivelling Platonic territory as reality made deeper and deeper incursions, he accepted the colonizer's rule as a fact and subverted it as best he could, by guile and deceit. He simply never did the things he did until they became plain as daylight and he couldn't deny them. Then, as he was about to be beaten, he'd yell, 'Have to do wee-wee! Have to do wee-wee!' The younger ones learned from him, and sang the same chorus as the blows began to descend. But sometimes they were so terrified of my father or Barbara that they really did wet themselves.

'Big Din-Din wants to be molly-coddled. You have only to look crooked at him and he's off into a stook,' Anthony would say when my father went upstairs to mope on his bed. But rather than worrying like the rest of us about my father's bad mood, he availed of these occasions to absent himself from the house, from the back yard, from homework, and go to the Fair Green, to meet Tarzan Kenneally and his buddies, council estate children old before their time.

I, however, had a fatal predilection for the official version of the way things were. My true perceptions of reality were always fleeting. I didn't understand what people and situations were really like because I had been told they were otherwise, or wanted them to be otherwise. On the huge portals of my inner world my true perceptions knocked – inaudibly. What was that sound? Did I hear something? No, it was the wind.

Boys in the town used to wear Cub badges in those days. A golden badge, like a golden button on a uniform, embossed with the word and a boy's face. It was a badge of distinction and I wanted one. When I wrote away for it, the

40

reply said the official golden badge was out of stock. A tin red badge was enclosed as a substitute. But I was also informed about a sign I could make with my fingers to another Cub, a sign which he would immediately understand as a request for a loan of his golden badge and, in Cub's honour, have to comply. But the other Cubs I approached didn't know what I was doing, making signs like that in front of their faces. They looked at me as if I had two heads.

⌁

Anthony knew that a puppet show was a puppet show no matter who pulled the strings: be it my father, or Stalin, or the short little solicitor by the precise clack-clack of whose heels every morning down the wide pavement you could time your watch, or de Valera, or the Devil himself. My first brother knew that the puppet show was the whole world, that the whole world was a puppet show, that big puppets pulled the strings of smaller puppets all the way down to us cooped up after dinner in the back yard, where we pulled one another's strings, in descending order, until the only one left with no string to pull was the youngest. My first brother may not have known it in so many words, but he knew all the same and he wanted to cut the strings right from the start.

There were some puppets who were pulled by more than one set of strings. My father pulled my mother's strings, but another set attached to her was pulled by the customers in our shop with their mounting uncleared accounts: *Six sliced pans,* said Sadie Kenneally, *two pound of rashers, four pound of sausages, eight pan rustics, a pound of tea, three pound of butter, two stone of spuds, three heads of cabbage, a two pound pot of raspberry jam and half a pound of bull's eyes isn't it a grand day entirely Mam and how is the Master?*

Oh, but the advent of the sliced pan! It must have been around this time that the saying began to circulate: *the greatest thing since the sliced pan.* And to me at the time, the sliced pan really was the greatest thing. It wasn't the labour-saving aspect admired by housewives and the ravenously hungry which attracted me. It was the taste. Of the first sliced pan I ever tasted, that came from Waterford. Called *Gold Crust.* Now I know that its unique taste probably came from additives, flavour-enhancers. The local baker couldn't compete with it: everything else was right, the coloured wrapping, the even slices, the price, but the taste was not right. *Gold Crust* was triumphant; after it, eating the local sliced pans was a bit like eating paper.

So what was the taste of *Gold Crust?* Something new at a time of life when the taste of food was everything, at the age of seven or eight. Something impossible to describe: *particular in the intransitive sense,* as Wittgenstein would have expressed it. Intransitive, intransigent to description, the taste-memory is a kind of transparent curtain behind which other memories act out the dumb-show of my child-hood.

Gold Crust came from Waterford with hopes of a changing world. The invention of the sliced pan was followed by the launching of the Sputnik into space. I was staying at my maternal grandmother's at the time; she needed company, and I, the eldest of the children, was providing it. A twenty-minute walk took me from our shop in the centre of town to her cottage on the hem of the countryside. This duty lasted for about two years. The first year was before I progressed into the higher classes which my father taught, and it may have been during this year that the radiant photograph was taken. Not only did I not provoke his anger by my apparent stupidity in class but I wasn't annoying him at home like the others, who would sneak down in their vests in the early morning to steal sweets from the shop or fight after dinner in the back yard or need to be walked for hours before going to sleep. For a while, the curly-headed stranger was held in high regard.

The taste of *Gold Crust* is the taste of hope. At this time my father still had hope. *The Amateur Photographer* had published his photograph of the Christmas crib in the friary chapel; he was gradually building up a portfolio of published photographs. He had opened 'The Quality Photographic Studios' (the parlour was his one and part-time studio), and some locals had even gone to him to have their photographs taken. He photographed donkeys with their churn-laden carts tied to telegraph poles outside bars, outside the stores of the Co-operative Agricultural and Dairy Society.

Except for the painter who later became famous, with whom he sometimes had long conversations on the street, my father was probably the only person in the town to see the wonder and potential of those everyday street scenes. The people of my home town were locked into the everyday as into a prison. For them, there was no epiphany in

43

the sight of a donkey and cart tethered to a telegraph pole, nothing about the bowed head of the donkey, the sad depths of the one eye in profile that, in the words of Roland Barthes, could *pierce*.

But in that town nothing pierced or could pierce; nothing could pierce the petty status hierarchy (the clack-clack of the solicitor's shoes) or the dumb purgatorial other-worldly faith which enveloped the bright potential of life here below like a grey perpetual mist (we must all suffer, but some must suffer more than others, so that the others may suffer less). Nothing could pierce the cynicism of a neglected town or the definition of the town coined by one of its many wits in a parody of the Catechism's definition of Purgatory: *a place or state of punishment where some souls suffer for a time before they get the money to go to England.*

The 'working classes' seldom had work in the town of my childhood. It was situated in a geographical and political no-man's-land, overlooked by whatever few development initiatives were on offer at the time. What *was* on offer, in the absence of enough money to go to England? The Great Sliced Pan in the Sky, the Sputnik Gold Crust circling the earth out of reach of present needs and dreams. That and the parish's Party for Poor Children, announced off the altar the Sunday after Christmas, with a curious addendum to the effect that *children are requested to bring their own cup, plate, knife, fork and spoon.*

It was mainly working-class people who shopped with us. We still kept credit notebooks for our customers at a time when the practice was going out of fashion with other shopkeepers. The bulk of our customers came from a council estate that had recently been added to the town. The estate was officially named after a patriot, people originally called it the New Houses, and it was later nicknamed the Burma Road (after the war film of the same name). I remember it as an area always strewn with broken glass. My father, another outsider of the caste system, though for a different reason, had a kind of sympathy with my mother's customers; he often talked and joked with them, he appreciated the cutting edge of their wit. Indeed if there was anything in the town of my childhood that could pierce to the heart of things, it was the cutting humour of its working class, as evidenced by that Catechism-parody definition of the place itself. I imagine one of the current wits of the town looking at my father's photograph of a donkey tethered to a pole outside the Co-operative Stores, and saying to me: 'Begod now, Ciaran, you'd want to airbrush the hape of shite out from under the ass's hindquarters before you put that photograph on exhibition.'

Sadie Kenneally, with her *six heads of cabbage, two stone of spuds*, and part-payment of her ever-increasing bill, would banter with my father in a salacious way, and he loved it. 'Go way, ya ould divil ya!' she'd say, and he laughed till the tears came down his cheeks.

'And six sliced pans, Missus. Gold Crust, if you have them.'

᠊᠊᠊

On creamery mornings, ours was a town of donkeys and carts. The queue stretched from the creamery entrance, down West Street to the Cross, where it described a right angle and continued up Main Street, past our shop. There were lively exchanges between the drivers of the donkeys as they waited in the queue; these often took the form of boastful predictions about the outcome of the next hurling match between the county where I lived and the adjoining one, whose border was just a few miles down the road, and from where many of the creamery carts had set out.

But above all for me on those creamery mornings, ours was a town of donkeys with sad, patient eyes; a town of churns mounted on simple wooden carts. Those were the reins, which the driver tugged every time there was a move in the queue, pulling on the bit in the donkey's mouth. Those were called *winkers*, the blinds ensuring that the donkey could look only straight ahead. And underneath was the *bellyband*.

A funny name that: *bellyband*. The lads on the Burma Road applied it to an item of women's underwear, the suspender belt for nylons. *I could see right up to her bellyband*, Anthony said to me once, describing how he had looked up a woman's dress as she lay on the grass of the Fair Green in the heat of summer.

There was something forbidden and fascinating about knickers. The solicitor lived near my grandmother, and I was invited to his son's seventh birthday party. There I met Harriet, who wore a pair of long pink knickers. They came to elasticated ends just above her knees. Harriet was pretty; she had a suntanned, slightly freckled face and long, dark-brown hair. She talked to me for a while and I remember feeling an odd sensation as she moved across the room, revealing her pink knickers through the vertical slit in her tartan skirt. The sensation left a lingering mysterious fragrance. There was a kind of holiness about the way Harriet moved, so that the unintentional revelation of that pink under the tartan almost took the prurient mockery out of the word *knickers*. I wished there had been another word for what Harriet wore.

It was strange that girls had no gillies. They had a kind of slit instead. My sister standing up naked in the bathtub, looking odd without a gilly. But Harriet was different. Harriet spoke to me. She spoke to me for a good while, and it was different from talking to boys, but still natural. Harriet made it seem natural for me to talk to her.

Harriet, too, was a different kind of name. But it suited her very well.

Afterwards, the solicitor's son wanted me to show him my gilly. He brought me round the back of their big house. *If I show you mine, will you show me yours?* I agreed out of good nature, but it didn't seem any kind of big deal. For the solicitor's son it was obviously an act of great import, this mutual revealing, but to me at the time it was just odd. I wanted to play hide-and-seek or cowboys.

The solicitor had a swimming pool, the only one in the locality. He also had lawns in front of his house, with monkey puzzles and other strange kinds of trees around the edges, and a driveway up the middle. There was also a big garden at one side, a fruit garden, and a vegetable garden at the back. In the fruit garden, there were raspberries, trained up an arrangement of cane sticks. The taste of raspberries was like the fragrance of Harriet, a dark fleeting kind of sweetness, a taste like a memory of a different world.

Raspberries stained my fingers. The taste of raspberries, of Harriet, spread like a stain over my mind. But it wasn't the kind of stain you get a hiding for; it wasn't like the stain of cowdung I got on my Confirmation suit, for which Barbara gave me the biggest beating of my childhood. It was a good stain, the kind that a painter tries out and is delighted to find that it works beyond all his expectations, setting up all kinds of reverberations and possibilities in his work. It is strange that a memory stain from such a tiny fruit, from such a brief encounter, should spread so inexhaustibly over the years. The twist of a girl's sweetness, of an intransitive taste.

What draws me back to this memory of Harriet is the aura she had of coming from a different kind of childhood, a lived childhood rather than one spent in external or internal retreat. She bore herself in the world with a confidence in what she was. She didn't have to hide in her dreams; they were hers to be realized. She didn't have to scatter them; they would come true in good time.

↩

It seems as if it was always February in my childhood, and I was a dreamer looking out a classroom window. Failure to concentrate got me in big trouble with my father. The dreams intervened between mathematical problems and their solutions, between the first-person singular and the third-person plural of the habitual pasts of Irish verbs. My father slapped me on the head, over and over, in front of the assembly of my peers. I was marked out for punishment because I was supposed to shine before the class; the Master's son had to be superior to the others. But I couldn't disengage myself from my inner world. The dreams in my head were assailed with blows, but they wouldn't budge.

I looked out the window at the cumulus clouds. It was sunny for once, but the clouds were building up, mounting, spreading. If I turned to look at the Master, the shape of the clouds had changed when I looked back out the window again. How could that be when they seemed so solid? Cumulus clouds, climbers, reachers for the sky. They were the Good Giants, they filled me with awe. But they could turn nasty, those ones: cumulo-nimbus. Lightning could come out of them and strike you dead.

They formed out of nothing and they grew and grew. They were dense, thick; they looked as solid as limestone and yet they were only vapour. You could walk through them if they descended. But they had a force inside them, great pressure in there – turbulence, it could shake an airplane to bits. But they looked so majestic. Was that what the end of the world was going to be like? You wouldn't be frightened at all, just overcome with wonder, as you are now by clouds, growing and swelling, huge dense clusters rising out of nowhere.

I was looking out the window learning Geography when I should have been looking at the Master and learning History.

And I was also dreaming one day as my father conducted a dictation lesson for the very first time. I came back to reality in time to hear him announce *My dog cut his*

49

leg on an open tin. I was bewildered, because we didn't have a dog. I searched wildly about in my memory, but no dog appeared except Clover, my grandmother's dog, who had mysteriously disappeared, but who had never cut his leg on an open tin. Could my father have had a dog I never knew of, maybe before I was born? But why was he telling the whole classroom about it now?

By the time I realized what was happening (the others around me were frantically writing down every word that came from my father's mouth), the lesson was practically over: the leg had been inspected, disinfected and bandaged, and the dog was lying comfortably in a cushioned basket.

In the perpetual February of my childhood, the land outside the classroom was visibly growing greener (towards adulthood?), but the general conditions were unpropitious. Branches of trees flailed in a continuous gale-force westerly airstream. The sky was covered in a moving mass of grey cloud that managed to lower even as it scudded. Great swathes of water flung from these clouds splattered against the window and created instant pools in the playing field, then the volume of rain would diminish to a perpetual downpour. Suddenly a living creature appeared on the screen of my daydreaming: a goose running to keep up with the wind, flailing its wings, the day's epiphany.

The westerly airstream boomed and buffeted and whistled against the solid stone walls of the school, and my father raised his voice in competition. The lesson in Irish History needed to be brought to a proper conclusion. Justice had to be done, though the heavens fell.

'And so we see how the Irish betrayed one another and let the Normans in to conquer them because of their petty jealousies and their bickerings. The big problem with the Irish throughout their history was that they couldn't unite. We saw that the one time when they did unite, they achieved a tremendous victory against the Danes at Clontarf. But as soon as the Danes were gone, they fell back into their petty squabbling again. And so on and so forth until we come to 1921. At that time, inspired by the bloody sacrifices of Pearse and MacDonagh and the other great leaders of 1916, the Irish looked like they would unite again at last and expel the English for good. They had it within their grasp, but at the last moment, what did our leaders do? They fell to squabbling and bickering again. And that is why, today, we have a twenty-six county instead of a thirty-two county Republic. We lost the North because we couldn't stay united. *In ainm an Áthar agus an Mhic agus an Spioraid Naoimh. Amen.*'

⌒

I didn't know much about westerly airstreams, but when I lived with my grandmother I became interested in orbits. A funny word *orbit*. I was living at the dawn of the space age, and besides the great Gold Crust in the Sky, there were soon to be bits of metal, known as satellites, circling the earth.

I thought an orbit was a hole in a kind of crust up above the earth, that sealed in earth and sky from outer space. Rockets and spaceships had to aim at these holes or else they wouldn't get out. I don't know how I reconciled this idea with the fact that the moon and sun, which I knew to be in outer space, could be plainly seen.

Looking at a photograph of a lunar crater in *The National Geographic*, I decided that it must be a hole in some kind of crust up above the sky; and having read a paragraph underneath the picture, which mentioned the word *orbit*, I concluded that the word was the name for this kind of hole. I explained about orbits to some friends of my grandmother, and they pronounced that I had plenty of brains and would go far. One of them said I would write great books for the Church when I grew up.

The Church came into the equation because it was commonly assumed I would be a priest; wasn't I an altar boy in the friary, and didn't I play at saying mass? What they didn't know was that I also played an auto-erotic game in front of the wardrobe mirror in the big bedroom at my grandmother's; but to me at the time, it was an enactment of Jesus being stripped of his garments. I ended up gazing fascinated at my body in the long mirror, naked except for my grandmother's dish-cloth around my private parts. Jesus on the cross was similarly clad in the huge Titian-esque painting in the parish chapel.

Anthony was quite the opposite to me in all these matters. Officially an altar boy, he seldom turned up for evening devotions, spending the time instead with his cronies on the Burma Road. And he just didn't get up in time for mass. His nascent eroticism was directed outwards, even if it was no more than a penchant for lifting girls' skirts. And he had little time for outer space or indeed for anything at all educational.

When the time came for Anthony to go to secondary, my father sent him to a school in the city, about ten miles away. He left every morning on the local bus. After a few weeks, my father decided to call at the school and see how Anthony was getting on. But he had never once attended; the headmaster had assumed that my father had changed his mind about where to send him.

I grudgingly admired my first brother's attitude to our domestic tyranny. It was courageous and at times gave us something to laugh at, the release of laughter's complicity. But his attitude was born of despair. And I believe that underneath the *sang froid* his anger grew, contorting itself in his teenage years into an admiration for Hitler's Germany, his bedroom walls covered with cut-out photographs of Panzers and Messerschmitts, of Hitler himself and Goebbels and Himmler, and big headlines proclaiming *Führer* and *Blitzkrieg*. Should the earth be laid waste again by war to atone for a bad childhood?

∽

My maternal grandmother always said 'God bless us' when anybody sneezed. A sneeze was an event that in some mysterious way demanded an evocation of the divine protection. Later, I learned that the French for *to sneeze* was *eternuer,* and I speculated that the word might originally have carried the meaning 'eternalize'; there being some danger that the soul, or some portion of it (if it could be divided), might escape through the nose into the next world in the act of sneezing. And if I shivered involuntarily, my grandmother explained the occurrence by saying that someone had just stepped on my grave.

Comparatively speaking, a sneeze was an important event in my grandmother's day. There was so little else: the daily rituals of eating, baking wholemeal bread, reading the paper, listening to *Mrs Dale's Diary* ('a recording of the daily happenings in the life of a doctor's family') and *The Archers* ('an everyday story of country folk'); feeding the hens, reciting the rosary, hanging the washed clothes on the clothes-horse that was lowered from the ceiling and hoisted up again by means of a pulley. A man used to call every week with goats' milk: this treat came in a tiny bottle that formerly had contained the stronger medicine of whiskey: a 'Baby Powers' bottle, stoppered with rolled-up newspaper. The man would stay chatting for a while, but little changed in the conversation from one week to the next except the particular event that provided the focus for ritual denunciations of the modern world. Whatever the event, it was proof that the world was 'gone to the dogs'. The event was always 'a fright' or a 'holy terror', or even 'a fright to God' or 'a holy terror altogether'.

My grandmother considered that the Irish weather, too, had gone to the dogs. It wasn't the same as it used to be. With perhaps uncanny insight, she'd remark, 'It's all them atom bombs they're exploding.'

At this time of her life, she no longer attended funerals, but she would sit at the window, the chintz curtain pulled slightly back, and count the cars as they passed her front gate on the way to the cemetery. The number of cars at any funeral was an index of the esteem in which the deceased was held. She would often muse aloud, when a funeral had passed, about how small or big it was, the consensus about the deceased's stature being at odds with her own. She ended these sessions of vocal rumination with some remark to the effect that there was no accounting for people, that the world was a funny place.

My grandmother was a grim woman, in the mould of her generation, who had witnessed the Black and Tans and the Civil War, in whose memory the Famine loomed large from childhood stories, a fairly recent occurrence. She was grimly satisfied with her life: she was never hungry, she had the electric light and the radio; even the solicitor, who lived just up the road, paid his respects to her by bringing an occasional pheasant. I have the impression that (in the words of Beckett) she was *content, necessarily*. She had memories of harder times, and even if her old age was a prison, it was (like Hamlet's) a *goodly prison*. In her circumstances, not just in old age but throughout her life, to express discontent would have been to fly in the face of God and man. Those who *had* more were to be shown the respect due to their station, but those like my father who *aspired* to something better were foolish, and indeed to be despised. There was a respect that came from accepting one's lot; that was why the solicitor brought pheasants to my grandmother. He was telling her that in one important respect she was equal to him: neither of them wanted to change their status or in any way interfere with the social order. But my father had critical ideas about the petty hierarchy of this town in which he was the merest blow-in, and that was why my grandmother didn't get on well with her son-in-law.

Once (and once only) I ventured to confide some childish disappointment to my grandmother, one that I cannot now remember – maybe a broken toy, maybe the episode of the Cub badge that wasn't a real Cub badge. 'How badly off you are,' she said, with regal severity.

For all that, my grandmother eventually became a refuge from the turmoil of my father's unsatisfied mind. There was a stability about her. It wasn't the kind of adult security before a child that helps the child to open out; but at least she didn't make hostile forays into the world of my dreams. I half-watched her, night after night, playing games of 'Patience'. There was a reassurance in the way the cards were eventually compelled into order, each suit laid out on the table in unquestionable compliance, King down to Ace, Ace up to King. This achievement must have soothed my grandmother, too, confirming her own belief in an unshakeable dispensation. She taught me to play 'Twenty-Fives', and it was easy playing with her; after all, my mistakes were to her advantage. If she was losing despite my inexperience, she'd get up out of her chair and walk round the table, to change her luck. Playing cards was a soothing ritual before bed. It resolved nothing, but kept things nicely on hold, and underneath the rituals my dreams were safe.

One day I told my grandmother that I wanted to become a priest. After some silence, she remarked, 'Ah sure, you're right, boy. There's nothing in the world.'

And sure what could there be in the world, when your father is angry and tormented, and himself and his buddy the housemaid are beating the daylights out of you, and de Valera wants things to stay the way they are, and masses are being said all over Ireland for the survival of Stalin, because you'd never know what kind of greater monster could come after him, and no prayers were ever offered up at all for the survival of your childhood?

4

The sea-area forecast

In the absence of a father-hero, I suppose I had to identify with some godlike male. That's how it goes with boys. My maternal grandmother read the *Irish Independent,* and the drama of *The Flying Enterprise* was headlined there day after day. A ship was in trouble out in the Atlantic, and had managed to keep afloat despite an increasing list. Thirty-five degrees, forty degrees: I forget the precise angles of inclination that were reported. The bravery of the captain fired my imagination. I don't recall his name, but his despatches from a worsening situation were conveyed to the nation daily and nightly, on newspaper and radio. My grandmother carried her chair over to where her wireless sat on a cabinet, putting her ear right up to it because she was a bit deaf, constantly adjusting the wavelength knob for greater clarity of sound. I listened too, either to the radio itself or my grandmother's summary. It was my first media-orchestrated vicarious adventure; I loved that heroism out on the stormy ocean. I loved it, too, because it was *something happening,* and I'm sure much of the population of 1950s' Ireland followed the drama of *The Flying Enterprise* for the same reason.

In the 1950s, the age of chivalry, or at least of its maritime equivalent, hadn't yet entirely passed. As I remember it, the captain of *The Flying Enterprise* reluctantly allowed himself to be rescued only just before his ship sank. But there was another drama to follow, on the Irish Sea, where a noble captain actually went down with his ship.

It must have been around this time that my father told me of the art competition. I painted a picture of a ship at sea. In the beginning it was just another ship at sea, and the sea was calm. I was working with real watercolours, in *tubes*, not the kind of ready-made children's palette that comes in a tin.

My father the photographer was also passionately interested in art. He never practised it, but had obviously intended to, because he had stocked up with boxes and boxes of all kinds of paints, with supplies of art paper and an imposing set of brushes, with volume upon volume of handbooks on *How to Draw, How to Paint, Painting with Watercolours, Painting with Poster Colours, Landscape Painting, Portrait Painting* and so on. He also had a series of editions covering the entire history of art. The man that my father talked to for hours in the street went on to become a famous painter, but my father stayed teaching and bored us about the sacrifices he was making for us.

A few years ago, my wife gave me a present of a book on the famous painter, and I was happy to see included in it a photograph my father had taken of the painter's aged mother. The photograph was clearly acknowledged as my father's, and placed opposite a similar portrait by the artist, so that photograph and painting reflect off one another. I was pleased by the now-famous painter's acknowledgment of my father, who was probably the only person who had anything in common with him in that small town in 1950s' Ireland. When I put the discovery of this excellent photograph side by side with my father's rantings and ravings about the sacrifices he was making to give us decent prospects in life, or whatever it was he thought he was giving us, I really don't know what to think. Was the famous painter brave, and my father not? Was the painter prepared, if needs be, to go down with his ship, and was that why he arrived on the opposite shore? Was my father shipwrecked on the notorious rock of sacrificing his ambitions, his talents, for his family, and hating them for it afterwards?

Two years before he died, I was in a pub having a Christmas drink with my father. Uncharacteristically, I was confiding in him – about my manuscripts coming back to me, rejection slip after rejection slip, and how discouraged I felt. Suddenly he gripped me by the hand and said fervently, over and over, 'Don't give up. You mustn't give up.'

Gradually, as my painting for the art competition progressed, the ship was covered with the turquoise of an engulfing sea. A spumy impasto flecked the mountainous waves. Eventually, nothing could be seen of the ship but the top of the mast. *Don't give up. Don't give up. Somewhere there's a port.*

I was always a solitary child. Staying with my maternal grandmother, I grew jealous of my solitude. So much so that I resented visits from the other children of our family. On Saturdays, my parents sent them to play with me. Looking up the road towards the town on Saturday mornings, I'd see them progressing in single file, four and later five of them, on the footpath, coming to invade my solitude. 'Bah!' I'd exclaim. It was an expression I had learned from English comics.

My grandmother sent us out into the field behind the house. We played 'Tig', but that soon palled. Anthony always got us up to some mischief such as chasing cows or breaking sticks from the hedges to play at swordfighting. The cows stampeded, or someone got a wallop of a sword on the legs or knuckles. My grandmother sent the others home. I watched them retreat up the footpath towards town, in single file, and returned to reading *The Beano* or *The Dandy*.

Desperate Dan ate cow pie. It was a pie shaped like the steak-and-kidney pies my aunt used to make, only it was much, much bigger. It must have contained an entire cow, and that was how it got its name. It wasn't just a steak pie or a beef pie, but a whole cow pie. Even the cow's horns were there, sticking up out of the crust as a decoration. Desperate Dan was enormous, with a chest like a barrel, and he had a huge protruding chin with a perpetual five o'clock shadow. He didn't know his own strength, and went around causing mayhem. When they saw him coming, little men jumped into dustbins. Just as the Mountie always got his man, Desperate Dan got his cow pie at the end.

Dennis the Menace was always up to mischief, but his father sorted him out in the end. Not that it made any difference. Next week Dennis would be at it again, causing more trouble.

Anthony was like Dennis the Menace. Barbara gave him that nickname, and it stuck for a while. It stuck until the day my father gave him a woeful leathering during a maths lesson, for not being able to determine the volume of a cylinder. After that he was nicknamed Volume.

⇜

Our shop on Main Street was named 'The Quality'. Apparently this was my father's idea. Other shops on the street had the names of their owners on the fascia boards, but ours was going to be different, not only as regards the quality of its merchandise and service, but in its quality name.

It was to be a shop for the quality, run by the quality. But ironically, in much the same way as a 'Select Bar' becomes a haven for drunks and down-at-heels, our Quality Stores attracted the poorer people of the town, the citizens of the Burma Road. There was a solid reason for this: credit. Under the counter, there was a notebook for every regular customer, into which purchased items were entered. At the end of each week, the customer made a payment, but there was always a balance left unpaid, and this deficit tended to grow and grow, until at last it became so embarrassing for many of the customers that they left us and went elsewhere, to shops which had a more stringent line on credit, or didn't allow it at all. Eventually The

Quality declared itself bankrupt; my father got a teaching job in Dublin and we moved there, my mother staying behind for a year to tidy things up. But in the early years of The Quality, there was an air of promise about the place.

There was something unique (even if not quite elite) about our shop. Many of our customers were so-called 'characters': Sadie Kenneally and her innuendo-laden teasing of my father; the shy little man who invariably wanted 'five Woodbines, two ounces of tea, a small pan and half a quarter of butter'; the dumpy little woman who was so busy, she told us, that she needed 'two elecktickity legs'. And the habitual drunk who, speaking to two elegant women who were waiting for the Dublin bus outside the shop door, broke off his discourse with what must surely be the greatest conversation-stopper of all time: 'Excuse me, ladies, while I have a piss'; and proceeded to pee down the leg of his trousers, so that the elegant ladies could see the stream running across the pavement into the channel beside the road, and the Dublin bus couldn't arrive fast enough.

The women who at one time or another assisted part-time behind the counter were young and attractive. Katie was afraid to go to the hut in the back yard which housed our one toilet in case Anthony would take advantage of her vulnerable position and play some trick on her – such as throwing water at her through the space between the top of the toilet door and the roof. Aileen was afraid of thunder and lightning, and would run upstairs to hide under the double bed.

Sadie Kenneally eyed my father eyeing our shop assistants. 'Ya ould divil ya. Haven't you the gamey eye?' she'd say. Aileen would ignore the innuendo with hauteur, but Katie would blush and attend singlemindedly to a customer, if one was available, or begin assiduously tidying the shelves.

Our shop was mainly a grocer's, but in time it became quite eclectic in its merchandise. My father's interest in music was reflected in the sale of guitar and violin strings and the sheet music of popular hits from Radio Luxembourg's Top Twenty: Woody Guthrie, Vera Lynn, Ruby Murray. We also opened a small lending library: a shelf was erected on the wall outside the counter and stocked with books from Foyle's travelling library. One day the parish priest dropped in, and my mother said she had just the book for him, producing *The Angelic Shepherd*, a pictorial biography of Pope Pius XII. 'I'd prefer an ould detective novel,' said the disgruntled pastor.

On Fair Days, we cleared the parlour and turned it into a restaurant. Farmers crowded in, leaned their knob-ended sticks against the walls or laid them on the floor under the tables, and sat crouched over large platefuls of bacon and cabbage or mutton stew, cooked and served by Barbara. The Fair Day catering was so successful that my parents decided to establish a permanent restaurant. The back room was sectioned into two by hardboard, to compensate for the family's forfeiture of the parlour. But the restaurant was a flop, except on Fair Days. One of our few regular customers was a mechanic, appropriately named Austin, who came for his tea. He arrived in his axle-greased overalls and smelt like the garage at the entrance to the Fair Green. I struck up a kind of companionship with him, fascinated by his smell and his aura of solitude. 'That's a nice lady,' I said to him, standing beside his regular table and pointing to the bathing-suited woman on the cover of his magazine. 'She's sprinkling her arse with the sand,' mumbled the shy man who smelt of car oil. I felt, obscurely, the offence of the word *arse* in relation to the nice lady.

At times our shop was like a small-scale Fair Day, with conversations flying, witticisms shouted across the counter, children being ordered away from the fridge and back into the yard, huddled groups laughing as they examined turnips or heads of cabbage, the whole business punctuated by the furious ringing of the till.

At other times, particularly during mid-week afternoons, it was quiet. I was sometimes asked to mind the shop after school. I sat in 'the Office': that was the grandiose name for the section inside the counter nearest the window. In this space, there was a partition of frosted glass erected on the counter, which meant you could sit in the Office and not be seen. I would sit there and read as the afternoon wore on and the street darkened outside the shop window.

Before I left for my grandmother's, I'd get a 'tuppenny wafer'. A block of ice cream was clamped by a rectangle of metal with teeth in it that marked out tuppenny sections. My mother cut a section off with a knife and placed it between two wafers, and off I went up the street, satchel on back, eating ice cream, heading towards my grandmother's in the failing light. In winter, it would be dark by the time I got to the edge of the town and the last streetlight. Afraid of the dark, I'd wait for the headlights of a car. When I saw headlights in the distance, I'd run as fast as I could, to cover as much ground as possible before the car passed and I was swallowed by darkness. If I was lucky, I had light or the promise of light all the way to my grandmother's. If unlucky, I was left floundering, my eyes unaccustomed to the dark because I had banked on accompanying light, in the middle of nowhere, with nothing to do but pray.

⤳

I was an over-sensitive child, I suppose, and hid in myself whenever I could. There was something very soothing in the way my grandmother laid the cards out over the table for her evening game of Patience. A peace descended on the living room. I was far from my father's and Barbara's threats: 'I'll clip your ear'; 'I'll beat you into the middle of next week'; 'I'll *manafooster* you'. The prospect of being beaten forward in time, offered by my father, sounded particularly terrible. On the other hand, the problem with Barbara was that she usually did much much more than just clip your ear. Manafoostering was also Barbara's department, but it was a menace associated with her more good-humoured days; she used it less to frighten than to humour us, because we thought the word was very funny. A colonizer's word, it was eventually adopted into our native back-yard language.

The cards were spread out over the table, my grandmother concentrated, and I sat across from her reading *The Beano*, or half-watching, half-daydreaming. Every now and then, some part of the house creaked, or a lump of coal split in the fire. 'There's a draught,' my grandmother would announce suddenly, and rise to close the window or put a cloth across the bottom of the front door. She was very nervous of draughts. They were known to have caused Pleurisy.

When the man with the goats' milk came, or his sister Aggie who worked in the kitchen of the solicitor's house, the talk was often of TB and Pleurisy, and of the people who had just contracted one or the other, or indeed both. 'She has TB and Pleurisy' is a sentence I clearly remember from one of those conversations. When people got really sick, they were sent to a place called Peamount. Draughts could cause TB as well as Pleurisy, not to mention ordinary colds and 'flu. My grandmother said 'God bless us' when somebody sneezed, because a sneeze was nearly always caused by a draught, and there was no knowing what a sneeze held in store.

But there was nothing worse than a Relapse. A Relapse was a condition much worse than the original illness, and it happened if you thought you were better when you weren't, and got up out of bed too soon. When they got a Relapse, people nearly always died from it.

My aunt, who often stayed with my grandmother on weekends, once brought me to the doctor, whose house was on the town side of the solicitor's. The doctor said I had 'a touch of Bronchitis'. I was rather proud, as if I had caught my grandmother and her friends wrong-footed, because they had never mentioned this disease. My Bronchitis gave me a new status. The next time the man with the goats' milk came, my grandmother pointed at me.

'He has a touch of Bronchitis, you know.'

'Well, the Lord save us,' said the man with the goats' milk.

With so much happening to people of her age, old acquaintances and friends, what was there for my grandmother to do of an evening only spread the cards out on the table and bring them to order? This little pack of fifty-two cards was one part of the world she could control. And peace descended on the living room as she arranged the cards. The silence was accentuated, brought into its own, by an occasional creak from the walls or a splutter from the fire, as the light from the window became a luminous pallor and the shadows in the room grew darker. Soon it would be time to light the oil lamp. (The electricity was still distrusted, and used sparingly.)

I watched a world of order taking shape under my grandmother's hands, and in this orderly world my dreams were free to wander.

⌐

Here is the sea-area forecast for 0600 hours:
Humber, Tyne, Fisher, Dogger, German Bight...
Cromarty, Forties, Fair Isle, Viking...
Malin, Hebrides, Rockall, Baily...
996 Millibars, rising slowly.....
1,023 Millibars, falling steadily....

Sometimes, waking early, I would catch my grandmother, ear to the radio, listening to the sea-area forecast. She would send me back to bed, but I stayed behind the bedroom door and heard the grave litany of weather stations along the coasts of Ireland and Britain, and the things that were happening there: wind-direction, wind-speed, chang-ing visibility, the fallings and the risings. I had no idea what they could be, those wonderful Millibars, and I did not imagine them as anything in particular. Enough that there was an even-toned voice reciting this solemn litany, that the sea was clearing to ten miles or five, that the wind and the Millibars were rising and falling. This sea-area forecast was one of the best poems I heard as a child, a beautiful half-comprehensible pattern of repeated words. For my grandmother, perhaps, it was a voice, someone that talked to her, filling the vacuous dread of insomniac old age. Or perhaps it was a mantra warding off the fear of death.

Shannon, Fastnet, Plymouth, Sole, Biscay, Finisterre …

One night I woke to hear my grandmother shouting, 'Ah God, I'm dying!'

I went to her room, where she was half-raised on the bed, leaning on her elbow.

'Water, water,' she said.

In the kitchen I got the big tin mug that hung from the wall on a crook, dipped it in the water crock and brought it to her. She raised herself up further, drank a few sips.

'That's all right, boy. Leave it there. Go back to bed.'

A horror clutched at my throat. I couldn't sleep.

964 Millibars, falling…

⌒

I was twelve when *King Solomon's Mines* arrived at our cinema. I badly wanted to see it, but there was no matinee, because it came in mid-week. How could I ask my father to let me go to the night showing? I didn't. I was on my way to bed when my mother told him how disappointed I was. 'But you should have asked me,' he said unexpectedly. 'I would have let you go if you wanted to see it that much.'

I believe *wanting things that much* became less important for me than fear of the pain of refusal or rejection the day of my father's infamous sentences. The ghost at the window of memory assures me that there was a time when I was quite capable of wanting things, and indeed getting what I wanted, and reminds me of the day I stole the half-crown from my brother Anthony's pocket.

Anthony was sitting in the desk in front of mine. We were still in the junior classroom, where the other teacher, Mrs Feehan, was haranguing us about the Sufferings of Christ, as she did for about an hour every day. (It was called the Christian Doctrine Lesson.)

It took several efforts, and a long time, to get the half-crown out of Anthony's pocket. Mrs Feehan brought a boy up in front of the class, laid her cane across one of his shoulders and then the other, pressing feverishly on the cane (but not beating him). 'They scourged Our Lord like that, on His Blessed and Holy Back.' There were flecks of spittle on Mrs Feehan's lips. Anthony leaned forward the better to see this re-enactment of the Passion, and my fist, gripping the half-crown, at last slipped unnoticed out of his pocket.

What a to-do there was about the robbery! I arrived at my grandmother's that evening, my four pockets bulging with bags of various kinds of sweets, my mouth crammed with liquorice allsorts. I offered my grandmother a 'black jack' toffee from the bag in my hand – the one I couldn't fit into my pockets. 'Hmmm,' I said. (It was how you said 'Here' when your mouth was full of sweets.) She refused the sweet and sat me down immediately in the armchair under the back window of the living room. I was interrogated, and sang. My hoard was confiscated and thrown out. I was reduced to a pathetic quiverer by the threat of bringing the sergeant down from the barracks. (An ordinary guard wouldn't do my grandmother; it had to be the sergeant.) Word was sent to my parents and I was interrogated again. I betrayed Anthony, who confessed that he had stolen the half-crown from the till.

'Haff to do wee-wee!' began Anthony, but surprisingly, my father took a fairly lenient view of the situation. He probably did so to spite my grandmother. But it has to be said that on rare occasions he showed a liberal streak. He couldn't tolerate the ordinary, everyday irritations that children cause, but sometimes managed to rise above more serious, isolated transgressions. We got off with a lecture on the evils of stealing.

The incident must have occurred sometime after my seventh birthday. My aunt had organized a birthday party at my grandmother's, and invited the solicitor and his family. I remember standing at the front gate, watching my parents and 'the lads' approaching on the footpath. The solicitor came over and pressed something into my hand, closing my fist on it. When I opened my fist, I beheld a large silver coin, embossed with the figure of a horse.

A half-crown was an enormous sum of money. The amount of sweets I was able to buy the day of the theft! My pockets crammed with them, and more than a shilling's change.

The next thing I remember from that birthday party is watching my family walking back towards town. The slump of my father's shoulders as he walked away from my birthday. They didn't seem to have stayed very long; the party was only beginning.

Had it something to do with the solicitor's half-crown?

⤷

Aunt Elly and Uncle Lar lived in Wexford, but they spent most weekends at my maternal grandmother's. They were childless, and would have liked to adopt one of us. I believe my parents considered the idea for a while: Anthony and myself, the two oldest, were possible candidates. Eventually, the idea was dropped, and my aunt and uncle adopted a girl through the usual channels.

During the time I stayed with my grandmother, I used to go to Wexford on short holidays. My uncle was a foreman in a meat factory. One day he brought me there and I saw a lot of friendly men in grimy overalls. He must have been a foreman in the maintenance division. The factory was a huge place, with all kinds of incomprehensible machines half-hidden in shadows. They made rhythmic thumping noises, but sometimes when you got to a place where you could hear them all together, the noise was chaotic and deafening. There was an oily smell, too. I remember getting a little bit sick.

My uncle was an authority on everything. Sometimes he met the solicitor at my grandmother's, and they discussed legal matters, such as 'the sin of neighbouring lights'. That's how I remember the phrase my uncle repeated over and over. This sin had something to do with growing your hedge too high, or not pruning your trees.

My uncle used to sit me on his lap, facing him, then suddenly spread his legs so that I fell. But he was holding me by the arms, and always pulled me back again just in time. It was a great thrill, that mixture of fear and fun. My father never did anything like that, at least not after we were able to walk: to be fair to everyone, he played with no one. My uncle used to tickle me under the ribs and say I was a Gilly-Gooley.

I liked my uncle and aunt. At times they could be severe, but neither of them ever hit me. Even my maternal grandmother beat me once. She beat me behind the legs with a 'switch', a thin pliable young branch from a tree or bush. I had stayed too late at the Horgans, a big farm about a quarter of a mile from her house. She was waiting for me in the middle of the road as I returned. The lashes of the switch stung into my calves and I cried. 'Galang outa that', she said. That evening at the Horgans was among the best of my childhood: one of the grown-up sons had taken me for a ride on the tractor. It was my first time on a tractor, but things had to end badly. Time had to be respected: it was an old woman standing in your road, wielding a switch.

The big boys up at the Horgans used bad language. They were always saying that things were 'scuttering this' or 'scuttering that'. Or that someone was a scuttering eejit or a scuttering bollocks. Cows were always scuttering: they left mounds and trails of scutter all over the place. The word fascinated me. You'd be a big boy if you used it. One Sunday morning at breakfast with my aunt and uncle, I pushed my plate of bacon, egg and sausages into the middle of the table, and said 'Ah, scutter!' I remember the shocked look of my aunt. She dressed me down severely, and my uncle gave me a talk on the importance of being *polite*.

My aunt and uncle were very polite. They always did the right thing. My aunt taught me what to do when I went to the solicitor's house. I should knock on the front door, rather than the back one, and when someone opened it, I should ask *Please may I play with Ray?*

> Please may
> I play
> With Ray?

Ah, scutter!

My uncle used frequently to caress my aunt, and murmur words of endearment to her. They were definitely ahead of their time in demonstrating affection to one another.

On one holiday in Wexford I remember waking up every morning with my eyelids stuck together. My aunt brought a bowl of cold tea to my bedroom, and gently applied a cloth soaked in it to my eyes. They opened. One morning they opened and saw snow falling outside the window. It was the first of May, I remember, and at first I thought the snow was apple blossom in the wind.

It was a fallen world, a rough world, I came into. Everyone was fundamentally flawed, but that didn't mean they were all *bad*. Some were good and some were bad, and there was so much good in the worst of them and so much bad in the best of them that it ill behoved any of them to criticize the rest of them. Many were stranded in a limbo between goodness and badness, living, as Dante put it, without praise or infamy: keeping their heads down, not sticking their necks out, making a quiet few bob. Some were *harmless poor ould craythurs who wouldn't hurt a fly.*

Martin, the farm labourer up at the Horgans, was one of these. He slept in a loft in an outhouse, but he ate in the farmhouse kitchen. I used to watch him eating his midday meal: two or three boiled eggs and two 'rustics' – V-shaped loaves I have never seen since my childhood, which came from the baker's in batches of six, but were usually sold in pairs. Martin drank strong black tea, plenty of it. He drank in silence, he liberally buttered his huge slices of rustic, he ate with utter absorption; his food was a territory over which he had total control, it could not be taken from him. He fed, not with the concentration of an animal, distracted by fear, but with the concentration of a man who was exercising his one and only unquestionable right: the uncontested right to food, needed to keep the body fit for labour. His meals were his property, his love and sex, the dreams that kept him going.

Martin left a deep impression on me. Perhaps I identified with him. Away from all my troubles in the silence of my grandmother's kitchen, I too crouched over my boiled eggs and rustic slices, similarly absorbed in the act of eating. My grandmother would pause from her comings and goings to watch me, grimly satisfied with my appetite.

⤷

The smell of boiled cabbage is the smell of my childhood. Cabbage thrown into the same pot as a pig's head and boiled for decades, for centuries. The fog in kitchens was cabbage-steam, the condensation on the walls was cabbage-flavoured. I was never completely free of that mild but all-pervasive odour, like a promise or foreboding that remained forever in a sort of half-existence, a dampening of the spirit or a mild elation. It filled not only my own house and my grandmother's, but every house apart from the solicitor's, where it was beaten down by the exotic aroma of ground coffee.

The smell of boiled cabbage is full of damp roads and hedges with a dull sheen of rain, of fields departing into mist. It is full of country cottages and aproned women bending in yards to feed hens or collect firewood. It is different from cabbage itself, the glistening robust heads on tough stalks in vegetable patches behind farmhouses.

The smell of boiled cabbage is sad and gentle, but it envelops you and you cannot escape it. *This is what you were*, it says: *a timid, inward child.*

The smell of boiled cabbage is fraught with modest expectations; it dreams of a holiday by the sea, the taste of the salt wind.

5

Wave-therapy

Holding me in his intent gaze, my therapist is telling me that my objection to his *ex cathedra* pronouncement about my father's sexual abuse of me is a perfect example of Freudian transference: I won't accept what he is saying, because I have unconsciously identified him with my father.

I don't know how to convince this therapist of the clarity with which I am able to distinguish between him and my father. I want to say that if it came to a choice between them, I'd prefer my father, because he at least was genuinely torn: his know-all attitude was a defence mechanism, whereas the therapist's is something more sinister, a closed system of absolute certainty from which, if I am sucked into it, there will be no easy escape. I push forward as best I can against the weight of my diffidence.

'You told me I was sexually abused by my father,' I say, 'and afterwards I have a dream that I am in bed with my father and he's sexually abusing me. Shouldn't it have been the other way around? Shouldn't I have had the dream first, before you made any pronouncements?'

'You have to trust me, Ciaran.' The therapist's tone becomes unctuous, almost pleading. 'Look at this piece of writing you have presented me with. You begin with the statement *The Almighty Therapist, the-rapist, the rapist, the mental rapist, is looking down on my unglorified arse.* And you proceed to heap all kinds of vilifications on me. Another classic case of transference: you are really expressing your feelings towards your father. *He* is the one who was looking down on your unglorified – ahem – bottom. And do you know what I connect that with, Ciaran? Do you remember that you told me about those auto-erotic episodes of your teens? You said that after masturbating, you lay on the bed and felt like Manet's Olympie? The painter, of course, was looking down on Olympie's naked body as he painted her. And her bottom, her nakedness, was *unglorified* because she was a prostitute. You felt you had been similarly degraded, Ciaran. Raped and mentally raped.'

I cannot accept this interpretation. I would have thought a phase of auto-eroticism was quite common, certainly not unheard-of, certainly not in a boy who was confined in a boarding school during his teenage years and hardly saw a girl from September to June. And as for my father, surely the physical and mental abuse was enough to achieve the state I'm in, without throwing in sexual abuse as well? But before I can muster the coherence to say this, my therapist continues.

'Ciaran, you must trust me here. In my practice I am constantly called upon to make judgments. Sometimes it is necessary to pre-empt things and point out a path which ought to be followed. You must believe me: I know from my considerable experience that you have all the symptoms of a sexually abused child. Trust me.'

'I don't trust you,' I hear myself saying.

'Ciaran, how could you trust anyone after your childhood experiences? But that's why it's so important now that you trust *me*.'

I won't be seeing him again: the limits of one therapist should not be the limits of one's world. But I will continue to have recourse to my long-standing practice of wave-therapy.

~

We stood in the water and screamed as a wave drove towards us. It was a delicious terror. On the seashore of West Cork we could scream all we liked; there was no one to shut us up. My father was a long way up the beach, photographing Barbara posed on a rock. Our screams were swallowed by the pounding of the surf.

The waves were called White Horses. They were horses with white manes. A cavalry suddenly appeared on the crest of a long ridge and spread out on both sides as it advanced. The army multiplied and charged into us. We withstood the first assault: perhaps the wave made you move a step backwards or forwards to keep your balance, but even as we steadied ourselves, another army was bearing down.

The waves are endless hordes of Barbarians, murderous on beautiful horses; we are spellbound by the beauty that comes with death, that bears it along. The killing cavalries crash against us and past us, wave after wave, until one comes that is so huge we lose our nerve and run, screaming, towards the shore.

There are bodies in the water on either side, a brother and sister struck down, but you are still running, and suddenly the chargers are docile at your feet, patterns of lace.

◡

The origins of my wave-therapy are to be found in those games we played in the sea during our summer holidays in West Cork. The ritual I have refined over the years would, I imagine, be classified as a species of aggression therapy (along with such other variants as the room that is said to be provided in Japanese factories where workers can go and vent their frustration by clubbing an effigy of the manager).

I devised my wave-therapy as an antidote to my mother's tea-ceremony. Standing in the waves is still great fun, of course; but now it is fun with a purpose. The waves are my father and my other misfortunes. Rather than taking the plunge immediately, I torture my body by gradual immersion in the cold water, thus allowing my curses and imprecations to gather slowly like an enormous thundercloud. A point of no return is reached when a wave slaps against my private parts: *you fucking bastard.* For fifteen or twenty minutes, I stand in the sea, taunting and vilifying the breakers as they crash against me and past me.

Cunt-wave, bollock-wave, fuck-wave, come on ya cunt ya, hit me again like ya used ta, wave after wave of ya, fuck ya, I may be battered and bruised but I'm still standin', cunt-wave, bollock-wave, fuck-wave!

Sometimes my wave-therapy takes more of a regressive direction, and I speak to the breakers in the whinging voice of a child who is about to cry:

You're a big wave and I'm only a little boy, and WHY are YOU trying to drown ME?

You're a Mastard, You're a Mastard, and that's ten times worse than being a Bastard, because there's ten letters between B and M. And you're worse even than a Mastard, you're a Zastard and that's the worst of all, there couldn't be anything worse than that.

One day at Spanish Point, I was distracted from my cathartic immersion by a beckoning figure on the shore, who turned out to be the lifeguard.

'Are we all right, sir?' he enquired in a wary tone.

⤸

Apart from the waves, and the fun of them, which I still enjoy today, transmuted into a therapy of catharsis, there were other remedial powers to be encountered during our annual holidays in West Cork. The strongest of these powers was to be found in the person of my father's mother, whom we called Granny-in-Cork. But the place itself, its landscape and seascape, had their own powers of enchantment to feed my memories and dreams.

The place seemed to work a spell even on my father. As soon as we had negotiated Cork city and were heading towards his place of birth and boyhood, he seemed to relax. He'd begin to tell us about things as we passed them, in an easy natural tone of imparting information, rather than the didactic preachy delivery he used in school, and the knowledge entered my memory with ease and stayed there.

'Do you see that long stretch of land out there to your left? That's a *peninsula*. It's called a peninsula because it has the sea on three of its four sides, from the Latin *paene* meaning almost and *insula* meaning island; almost an island.'

Peninsula. Looking out the car window, I see land stretching away out to sea, fading to an outline in sea-haze or coming to an abrupt end in cliffs crowned with a beacon or lighthouse. Peninsulas are full of *inlets:* when you turn a bend you suddenly see the sea again, seaweed-coated, sucking at the drystone breakwater on the road's edge, nothing but a funny kind of half-bridge (a parapet on one side but none on the other) between you and the Atlantic Ocean. Because that's what your father said: this little seaweed-bobbing inlet is a part of the mighty Atlantic Ocean.

The Ilen was a tidal river, my father explained; that is to say, the tide came in and out on it for a long way up. It wasn't tidal just at the *estuary*, like a lot of rivers; but there was, all the same, a certain point on it beyond which the tide couldn't reach. Around the point where the tide ended, beyond which the Ilen was just an ordinary river, the water was *brackish*, meaning it was a mixture of salt water and freshwater.

Everything is West Cork was a fascinating kind of mixture; it was a brackish kind of place where one minute you'd think you were surrounded by land and the next minute, if you weren't careful, you'd drive straight into the sea. The fields were brackish too: little patches of grass that would hardly graze a single cow, surrounded by acres of ferns and rocks. The inlet at Ballydehob, spanned by the famous twelve-arch bridge, seemed to be always brackish as between mud and water. And it seemed a brackish kind of thing to do, to build such an important-looking bridge over such an unimportant-looking inlet. Those were the brackish kinds of things the British used to do in their colonies.

And the air was brackish with the scent of heather and the tang of the sea, and the strong fragrance of turfsmoke was mixed in on the cooler evenings of those long-gone summers; and forever afterwards, that mingling of smells, whenever you sniffed it, seemed to conjure up West Cork, inlets and peninsulas and bobbing seaweed, harbours and villages and old railway cottages, montbretia and fuchsia on roadsides, small fields among rocky acres of heather and ferns, surrounded by the hugeness of the ocean and of the sky.

An image floats into my mind: we shin up the bank on one side of the twelve-arch bridge at Ballydehob and walk across it, tight-roping on the rusty-brown rails or hopping the sleepers. We descend on the other side, to a sandy beach imperceptibly lapped by a calm sea on whose glassy surface we skeet smooth stones. On reflection, I realize that in this image two distinct places have merged. There is no beach on the inlet spanned by the twelve-arch bridge, where the receding tide reveals expanses of mud; the beach I see in my mind's eye is not there at all, but six miles away, at the northern entrance to Schull.

Memories of pleasure coalesce, eliminating not only geographical and temporal distance, but also the boredom, the nothing-happening, even the pain that separates them from one another. This is the essence of nostalgia: striving to create in the past a place or state where all pleasures exist together.

⌒

I have a vague memory of being in a pub in West Cork with my father and some of our many relatives. I have never been much good at placing people in the lines of consanguinity and affinity; as soon as they get beyond being aunts and uncles and first cousins, relations disappear into an amnesiac fog and are never heard of again. For whatever reason, I see them as worse problems than quadratic equations or trigonometric reductions; second cousins are more difficult than cosines. Where have they come from, these people, and why are they here, claiming my time, or even a night's or a week's lodgings, as of natural right? My unconscious seems to take a perverse delight in confusing my friends' sisters with their sisters-in-law and their uncles with senior colleagues from work. Some old hatred of blood and marriage, and their hydra-heated ramifications, lurks within me.

In the pub there was a woman, a second or God forbid maybe a third cousin, bright and energetic, in her late twenties or early thirties. This cousin was 'nice', as we children said in those days, meaning both good-looking and kind, and a woman below a certain age couldn't possibly be one without being the other. (We would never have considered Barbara good-looking, because she wasn't kind.) Above that certain indeterminate age, a 'nice' woman was allowed to have wrinkles and other blemishes, as long as she was kind.

My cousin kissed me many times, and bought me bottles of Little Norah. That was a locally produced lemonade; the bottle had a label showing a young girl, red-cheeked and smiling, wearing an apron and some kind of headdress vaguely reminiscent of a nun's. She was carrying a tray of drinks. For some reason the lemonade was named after the girl; this act of naming wasn't as clear-cut as the naming of the Ilen, which anybody would know was quite obvious when he saw the islands in the middle of the river.

Despite Little Norah's shiny-clean tray of glasses filled with lemonade, there is a pervasive smell of porter in this memory, slightly decadent and disreputable (perhaps my father's mother had been sounding off in her harmless way about the evils of drink before we left for the pub). I remember a cheerful atmosphere. I didn't quite know what to make of getting all those kisses. They weren't *totally* annoying, even though I didn't have the kind of body that could respond easily to such attentions.

The only other thing I can remember from this pub-gathering, this meeting of kindred, is the allure of bottle tops; shiny, precious-looking, pieces of eight. I collected them off the floor as people talked around me, and put them in my pocket. They looked like some kind of money.

But I can imagine my father being his best expansive self that evening. He is, perhaps, meeting these relatives for the first time in years, and now he is a teacher, a man who has got himself a permanent pensionable job in hard times; comparatively speaking, an intellectual. He would have been asked about new ideas in education, and would have held forth on the topic, providing the soupçon of enlightenment that people expected from an educated man, a man of education, even though they knew enlightenment wouldn't work practically, of course, because the children would grow up spoiled if these new ideas were ever actually implemented. And my father, being not only educated and a bit of an intellectual, but also a man of the world and a sound Catholic, would have acknowledged the human nature factor, the lapsarian element, and everybody would have been happy with him and ordered another bottle of stout or pint of porter.

⤿

Granny-in-Cork, my father's mother, lived in a place with a name as funny as Timbuktu. In my home town up the country people used to say of someone who had disappeared off the everyday scene that he might as well be in Timbuktu or Ballydehob for all they had seen of him lately. Timbuktu and the place where Granny-in-Cork lived were equally unlikely places to be. (It must have been embarrassing for my father to have to tell people in my home town where he was from.)

My paternal grandmother lived in the end-house of a terrace off the main street of the village. The road she lived on could hardly be called a street, because there was no corresponding terrace on the other side, nothing but a few sheds, and directly across from her house there was a steep field with a huge backbone of rock where we often played at being mountain climbers. It was a kind of half-street or a small country road that wanted to be a street. (To this day, its ambitions remain unrealized.)

Granny-in-Cork's house was a cut above the others on the terrace because it had a small railed-in garden in front, whereas the other dwellers had nothing but footpath to greet them when they walked out their doors. But my grandmother's house wasn't the last edifice at that end of the village: a local handyman had erected an ugly corrugated iron shed alongside her, where he made or fixed things. My grandmother's house was built on rock: beyond her small back yard there was a sheer drop to the level of the harbour.

The people of West Cork had a funny way of giving directions; instead of saying 'Go straight ahead' or 'Turn left at the bridge', they'd say 'Go south the road' or 'Go west the road and turn south at the bridge'. It seemed that all these people had seafaring ancestors, the points of the compass were in their blood, and they were still pretending that they were on sea-roads rather than solid land-roads. In my county, people would say 'Stick to the tar' when they meant 'Stay on the main road', and in a way their feet were stuck to the tar or at least to the ground; they had no notion of what it was like to travel in that other, less dependable, more mysterious element.

To me, it was strange that people would talk of going south or west when the distance to be covered was quite short; unless, of course, they were lost in a wood. I had always thought that these were very large-scale, global kinds of directions and I associated them with major expeditions, such as setting out to find America. In any case, the whole business was completely baffling, because the people of West Cork would even say 'Turn the key south in the door'.

↜

Granny-in-Cork was full of old sayings and strange idioms and *ochón alannahs* and *alannah ochóns;* and *Ochón alannah* she said and stroked my hair one Sunday when I came back from mass and told her what a hard climb it was up to the church; and if she heard us squabbling, instead of clipping our ears she'd recite a poem:

> Birds in their little nests agree
> And what a shameful sight
> When children of one family
> Fall out and chide and fight.

And 'Dinny, Dinny, leave the children be' she'd chide my father, and she had some hold over him because in West Cork we were let do things he normally wouldn't allow, like climbing the rocks in the field across the road; and even Barbara, who usually came with us instead of our mother, had to restrain herself, and she must have had to sleep in someone else's house because we didn't see her until about ten in the morning when she'd arrive with a bag of sliced pans and ham for the sandwiches, and then Granny-in-Cork did the hardboiled eggs and my father made a show of supervising everything and checked his cameras and went out onto the road and held the light-meter up to the sky. And Granny-in-Cork fussed *alannah alannah*.

'Dinny, Dinny, come in and look at the cut on the child's shin.'

'It wouldn't have happened if you didn't let them out playing on the rocks,' says Dinny.

And Granny says 'Ah Dinny, they're only young once and a cut will soon heal, won't it?'

'As long as they don't break their heads,' says Dinny.

'Don't be always thinking the worst,' says Granny.

And Barbara wants to clip an ear or two but she has to keep her head down and butter the sandwiches, and Dinny wants to manafooster his mother because he can never get the better of her, she always has a word to cap his, and that's probably why he never let anyone else have the last word for the rest of his life.

And Granny-in-Cork fusses happily around, loving the presence of children, imagine, *loving* our presence, and giving us a good feeling about ourselves, and she washes the cut on the child's shin and puts on a bandage, and Dinny goes out in a bit of a stook and drives off in the car to get petrol for the day's journey to Barley Cove or Rosscarbery or Baltimore and lemonade for the picnic, anything other than being bested in front of his children by his mother, and he sits in the car when he returns and takes out his notebook and writes *Petrol 12s 6d, Lemonade 1s 0d,*

Sweets 1s 6d; totting up sacrifices for his defence at the Last Judgment.

⤸

Something in my father's mother flipped whenever she beheld us. She was smitten by that ultimate biblical blessing, *May you see your children's children,* and she couldn't stop fussing over the offspring of her son. A dance sprung up in her mind that didn't know how to translate itself into body; hers was a broken syntax of over-feeding and sudden embraces and readiness to call the doctor at the sound of a sneeze. Her continuous jumbled narrative of proverbs, verses and admonitions, half-understood by us or not understood at all, fragments of it remembered and most of it forgotten, has left behind it a sense of possible blessedness, as if someone passing down the street had shouted *There is another way!* in a foreign language, and the uncomprehending listeners noticed a sudden vibrancy in the air around them and felt a promise of better days rise in their hearts. Any even though we didn't know what precisely our grandmother's happy pother was all about, we were happy to know in some way that we were the cause of it.

90

6

Otherworldly eyes

I am in the dark of the con-
fession box; it is my first confession. The shutter slams back
and I try to speak, but my voice will not work. My mouth
moves, my throat moves, but no sound comes.

Tell your sins, says a solemn voice in the dark. At regular
intervals in the dumbstruck silence, *Tell your sins.*

The voice is not a friendly, coaxing voice. This is the command of an unfriendly God, who knows you have sinned.
You were conceived in sin, born with a sin on your soul, so
how could you *not* have sinned, even if you're only seven?

Over and over, in the weeks before that first confession,
I had rehearsed what I was going to tell. I had sins by heart
to mention, sins with long names, sins of omission and
sins of commission. Why, then, did my voice fail me? Who
was the God that struck me dumb? Why did no one inform
me that there was another God, within me, who would not
tolerate this rigmarole of guilt?

But Father Tell-your-sins won the day. The order of the
universe could not be disturbed. The cards were shuffled

and dealt, shuffled and dealt again and again, until the suits at last were four columns in perfect sequence on the table, Ace up to King, King down to Ace. I recovered my voice, and it mentioned a few technical transgressions.

'For your penance, now, say three Hail Marys. And a good act of contrition – *Oh my God… Ego te absolvo a peccatis tuis …'*

⁓

Father Tell-your-sins left his mark on me: in my confusion, I wasn't really sure if I had made a Good Confession, and Mrs Feehan had warned us about the depravity of making a Bad Confession. If you died after making a Bad Confession, your soul would go straight to Hell.

I had seen in the parochial hall a play about Robert Emmet's lover, Sarah Curran, produced by the nuns from the convent and acted by their senior girls. The play terrified me: Sarah Curran was portrayed as spending most of her time on her knees praying for a United Ireland, and being visited incessantly by the Devil, whose arrival was announced by a wooden clappers and lights going off and coming back on. The Devil's message for Sarah Curran was always the same: it was useless praying, England would win the day, Robert Emmet would be executed.

After my Bad First Confession, I imagined myself, dead, waiting in an ante-room of Hell. Suddenly the lights went off and on, the wooden clappers sounded their dry thunder, and the Devil jumped into the room, flapping his huge bat's wings, his eyes glowing red-hot coals of hatred.

'You're mine!' he croaked, and dragged me off to the deep dungeon where people went who had made Bad Confessions.

In those days, you had to fast from midnight if you were taking communion. Once, I ate something in the early morning, and I was so afraid of telling my maternal grandmother about it that I went to communion with her. It was a mortal sin, but I hadn't the courage to tell it in confession. For years afterwards, I kept my secret, implicating myself more and more in guilt every time I failed to confess it. Not that it troubled me at all times of the day and night, but it surfaced every now and then, convincing me that I would be damned. My guilt was something I couldn't reconcile with the rest of my life, but it was there. I asked indirect questions about it. 'Mammy, Auntie Elly, is it *really* a mortal sin to break your fast?' But the adults in my life always referred back to the teachings of the church, to *what the priest said,* washing their hands of the prospect that a child could eat something and be damned forever.

⌐

Clover, my grandmother's dog, had been put down for eating eggs from her henhouse: so my mother told me years later. At the time, my uncle said he must have wandered off and got lost. For days and weeks, I stood in a mystical cloud of sadness at my grandmother's back gate and watched for his return. I waited for his shape to appear at the far end of the field, and come bounding towards me. It was only a matter of time. But why then did the mystical cloud, the Cloud of Knowing, continue to envelop me as I stood there, watching the light and shade play around the gap in the corner of the field, expecting the sudden emergence of a more agile, vibrant shadow; a shadow that, as it closed the distance between us, would take on the substance of a floppy-eared collie? The Cloud knew; something had gone from my life unannounced.

Before Clover was put down, my grandmother had experimented with conditioning. I remember her standing in the kitchen, coaxing the dog towards her with an egg held out in one hand. The other hand, hidden behind her back, gripped a stout stick. I remember Clover's agitated sidlings towards her, eagerness fighting suspicion until his egg-addiction brought him near enough for my grandmother to strike one hefty blow, and he went yelping out to the yard and across the field.

That time, he did return. He cringed a wide circle round my grandmother as she gave him a verbal warning. But the conditioning was not applied consistently. The egg–pain association disappeared from Clover's mind, with the result that Clover disappeared from my life.

∽

I remember waking up in the middle of the night in my grandmother's one Christmas, hearing Uncle Lar's and Aunt Elly's voices in the living room, and a sound like that of a toy car racing across the floor. Excited as I was, I had to stay in bed, because Santa Claus was coming. He might get into a huff and not leave any toys for a child whom he saw up and about. I went back to sleep and on Christmas morning there were two racing cars in my stocking at the end of the bed, the kind that you wind up by creating friction between the back wheels and the floor or the surface of the table or any reasonably solid surface at all. 'Even the palm of your hand will do', my uncle explained.

I watched the back wheels spinning round in mid-air and listened delighted to the authentic engine-sound. But there was a question I couldn't suppress: why had my uncle and aunt been playing with the toys Santa had left for me? My uncle assured me that they hadn't; that I must have been dreaming.

It was wonderful that my dream had come true, but it was strange that I was only dreaming when I felt sure I was awake.

⤻

On the Feast of Corpus Christi there was a solemn procession of the Blessed Sacrament through the town. Shop windows had been emptied of their usual goods and stocked instead with holy pictures, holy statues and floral wreaths. Rosary beads of different colours, pearl ones and black ones, red ones and green, were strewn between the holy statues. Papal flags of gold and white, with the papal insignia of mitre and keys, were hung out of top windows. Out of some top windows, the tricolour also flew.

The procession began at the big chapel, passed down the main street, down the narrow street over the bridge, and finished in front of the convent, where a temporary altar had been erected. Everyone knelt before this altar, on the grass or (less fortunately) on the sharp chipped stones of the forecourt and driveway. The entire rosary, fifteen decades of it – Joyful, Sorrowful and Glorious Mysteries – was recited before Benediction. Some adults took out hand-kerchiefs to put under their knees; although they already had long trousers or skirts to numb the pain of the chips, they probably also wanted to keep the grime off their clothes. Children, especially boys, were well used to having their knees dirtied and cut; there was no fear of them.

I remember kneeling in the summer heat during those long prayers, shifting from one set of edged pebbles to another. The priest's voice intoning, and then the huge murmur of the faithful. The heavy solemnity of it all. The absent meaning of the raised golden monstrance, contain-ing the white host in its glass centre. Now I can understand the monstrance as a representation of the old sun god, with Christ appearing in the centre as the true meaning of that ancient pagan worship. But at the time, the sheer length of the festive devotions drained me of religious sentiment.

The old women joined in the hymns with the choir, their cracked, keening voices reaching triumphantly out of some timeless region of sorrow; a joy that sounded like misery. They mimicked the Latin of *Tantum Ergo* and *O Salutaris Hostia* to perfection, from hearing it over and over again throughout their lives. And the feeling they put into the incomprehensible words was all the more super-naturally religious because they did not understand them. They were being transported into the other world by singing in an arcane language.

I have a few photographs my father took of Corpus Christi processions. One of them shows the first-communicant girls – the pride of the procession, with their white dresses, tiaras and veils. Passing 'Harty's Restaurant and Dining Rooms' on the square, they are captured in some disarray. Most of them are craning their necks, staring at something to the left of the picture. Two in front are engaged in an argument with one of the 'stewardesses' flanking them, who is only marginally older, but distinguished by the darker shade of her dress. A child's concentration easily evaporated during those long-drawn-out rituals; perhaps the photograph shows a pause between the singing of two hymns.

⌒

In some deep part of me, I couldn't take the world very seriously. That was because I saw my grandmother killing hens. How could I take very seriously a world where an old woman would catch a harmless fowl and place it, fluttering and squawking, between her black-skirted knees, and saw the top of its head with a breadknife, up and down, up and down, until dark blood welled up through the plumage and the fluttering and squawking ceased? And then bring the dead bird in to the kitchen table and pluck it naked as a new-born babe, all goose-pimpled? And *gut* it, so that the entrails flopped out and slid over the table? And wash the dead bird in a basin of water clouding with blood, sprinkle it with salt and pepper and put it in the oven? And then clean the same table and set it for dinner?

How could you be in earnest about a world where humans had to kill other creatures in order to survive themselves? We had learned about blasphemy in school, what a horrible sin it was. But wasn't this killing of other creatures a kind of blasphemy inherent in the very nature of things?

I learned about cause and effect at my grandmother's because I witnessed from start to finish the process that culminated with eating. One good thing about returning to live with my parents was that I no longer had this disturbing perception: food did not come from anywhere in particular any more; it just appeared on the table and quickly disappeared again into six hungry mouths.

Because I couldn't take the world very seriously, I was always on the look-out for a replacement. Heaven, of course, was the perfect world. But there was one problem about Heaven: you had to die to get there. Another problem was that you had to be *very* good in this life to avoid Purgatory and go straight to Heaven.

The third problem I had with the idea of Heaven was that it seemed a very *spiritual* place, full of abstractions like eternal joy and everlasting happiness. Seemingly, the only concrete activity was a perpetual singing of hymns, and I probably associated hymn-singing with sore knees from the stones on the convent driveway.

'Mammy,' I once asked my mother, 'will there be any Kimberley biscuits in Heaven?'

'No, there won't be any, but we'll have no need of them' was her unsatisfactory reply.

O Angel of God
My Guardian Dear
To whom His Love
Commits me here
Ever this night
Be at my side
To light and guard
To rule and guide.

Above the painting of the Crucifixion behind the high altar in the parish church, there was a tableau of angels flocking round the all-hallowed head of God the Father Almighty. The angels were no more than little babies, but they had wings. They were little winged baby-heads.

Mrs Feehan told us that angels sometimes appeared on earth. Often they were disguised as beggars, like the one who met Tobias. If you refused an alms to a beggar, for all you knew you might be refusing an angel. Angels had been known to appear in times of great trouble; two of them were seen walking in the no-man's-land between the trenches during World War I. Angels were beings so full of light that you couldn't look straight at them unless they were disguised. But their light was full of happiness; even though you weren't able to look at them directly, you would feel the light of happiness basking on you in their revealed presence. That is, if you had given them an alms when they were disguised as beggars. Otherwise, the light would frighten you to death. Simeon died of fright in the heavenly light because he kept some of the church's money for himself. Ever after, keeping the church's money for yourself was called *Simony*.

The soldiers who saw the angels walking between the trenches saw them only because they had suffered so much. The angels you couldn't see without suffering a lot were called *angels of consolation*. When Jesus went through his Agony in the Garden, one of these came to console him. But Mrs Feehan said Jesus' sufferings were so great that the angel made no difference. His sufferings were so great that even God the Father couldn't console him, not to mind an angel.

That was the time when Jesus' sweat came out as drops of blood. It was the time when huge holes occurred in the universe and began to suck in the stars.

There were loads of pop songs about angels, but the angels in them weren't real angels at all; they were beautiful women. The songs were about *desiring*; that was a mood that came over a man when he saw a beautiful woman. And that was why the singers often said *Ou-ou-ou* in the songs, something you'd never say to a real angel. It was more like the sound an animal would make.

There were men from the New Houses who used to hang out every day down at the Cross, outside the Central Hotel or Harty's Restaurant and Dining Rooms. And every time a good-looking young woman passed them by, they'd make all kinds of growling noises, as if they were tethered dogs and she was a walking bone or a lump of mobile meat. These were the kinds of noises men made when they were desiring women.

The hairdresser was a very pretty woman. She painted her face, and she walked in a funny way. Suddenly she left the town and was never seen again. Anthony said she left because Jack Nickleby took her down by the river one day and 'did' her.

So many different kinds of 'dids': *Jack Nickleby did the hairdresser. Mammy did the washing. The Goog O'Shea did the football pools. Seán Hogan did Gusty Doran out of a fiver.*

And was my father desiring Barbara that day when he played the game of hip-butting with her in the kitchen? It gave me a bad feeling to be watching that game. It didn't seem like a right game for them to be playing, but I didn't know why. I couldn't add my perceptions together: my father not sleeping with my mother, my father hip-butting Barbara, my father taking Barbara away for long photographic sessions while we children waited in the car parked by some scenic roadside, my father always angry, beating us, Barbara always angry, beating us, my mother seldom seen, busy in the shop, showing us affection in a sad, discreet and fleeting way, my father not loving us, my father always elsewhere in his mind, the sullen way he ate his boiled egg, spreading his sullen gloom, enveloping us in his moody failure. Was this my father, and was this my life? And did it all happen because of the awful desiring that my father could not satisfy, a dog at the end of his tether, out of reach of the meat?

Something happened that autumn day, and it has never ceased to happen. A wound was opened that has continued to bleed its way through my life, the wound of childhood unhappiness. I wake in the middle of the night because the spirit-blood is seeping out of me, because the gash at the centre of my being demands attention. *Don't ever raise your voice to me again.*

Never, Father? Never, spoken by the Father. Father Never. You were never my father from that day. From that day, I began to look for another father.

Careless words that opened my life's wound. Children running in the falling leaves, and there was my corpse, my shadow, running among them. I was absent, I was elsewhere, I was not in my corpse, my shadow was not me, after that defining moment. Screen memory of an empty body running through autumn leaves, of a mouth without breath shouting.

Terrors infested the wound. It became a black hole into which the universe vanished. The autumn leaves in their golds and russets swirled round and round it and were sucked in, vanished beyond the event horizon. The so-whatness of spring flowers and April showers arrived and withered, evaporated, in the unanswerable question of my gaze. Because I was not loved. Because you did not love me. Never Father.

My shadow survived unhurt. It read *The Beano* and *The Dandy*, it ate my grandmother's boiled eggs and wholemeal bread.

Let there be no more fathers. All but one shall live.

Let there be no more bitter fathers, no more frustrated

men conceiving children as a matter of course. No more bitter Never Fathers putting out the lights of children's eyes with their careless words and insouciant silences.

Father, heal me of your absent love. I beg you, I implore you, I beseech you, make me whole again by one kind look from your otherworldly eyes.

⌐

The chapel was high and hollow and footsteps echoed. Every little sound was magnified, because these were important doings, no matter how small they might be. The audible sigh of an old woman wrapped in a black shawl, the clack of her rosary beads against wood. She was like the publican in the parable, away down in the second last pew; she wouldn't vouchsafe to come up further, because of humility. It was a lovely word, *vouchsafe*. I prayed that God would vouchsafe.

My footsteps echoed in the vast cavern of quiet. It was enough to genuflect on one knee, because God was not exposed. He was behind the golden doors of the tabernacle.

I arrived at the parapet of white marble which separated the sanctuary from the rest of the church. Standing beside it was the brass-gleaming trolley with its rows of candleholders. I put my penny in the slot and took a small candle from the nest. I lit it from another candle, placed it in a candleholder and knelt to pray.

Echoes of footsteps. Sighs and whispers. Telling of troubles. Small sounds that would not be forgotten by the silence which received them into its vastness. I was a quiet inward child who didn't know the trick of winning love. But I was safe in the place in my heart where God was, the place he had vouchsafed me. The little flame that burned before the high altar was for God to deliver me. My lovely God would deliver me from the wrath.

⟿

What an exasperating child, always in a dream, his responses so minimal, so unenthusiastic. It's as if his ice cream had to be sanctioned in the otherworldly realm; but a voice comes to him from the Cloud of Unknowing, which says: *There is another ice cream, not of this world. It is not limited to a few bites, its enjoyment is not circumscribed by the threat of envious snatching hands. It will not melt in the summer sun and stain your trousers, an eventuality which may earn you a hiding. It is not a nervous, looking-over-the-shoulder pleasure. The Ice Cream in the Cloud is the Host of Forever, which will not be taken away.*

⟿

My mother is sitting with me in the parlour, asking me a quiz from *Ireland's Own*.

'What is the most popular Irish boy's name?'

'Emmanuel', I reply confidently.

I had just heard from a priest in the friary that it was the biblical name for Jesus. It *had* to be the most popular name, because it was Jesus' name. That practically no one in Ireland had ever been christened Emmanuel was quite immaterial.

'What's wrong with you?' my mother demands. 'It's Patrick, of course.'

That's the kind of child I was: the obvious escaped me. I lived in a world that had laws of its own.

⌒

I look back at how dour and uncommunicative we all were, each of us huddled in on himself for protection, trying to cope with his life as he found it, maybe trying to preserve and nurture some remnant that might survive into the future.

This inwardness and dourness was highlighted by a visit from our American cousins. The gap in assertiveness between us and them was almost comical. One day as we were walking to my grandmother's, Cousin Liz, having tired of looking around her and inviting us in a general way to *Gee! Look at those cows* and *Gee! Look at that donkey*, made a brave effort to engage one of my brothers in conversation.

'Are you going to the party?' she suddenly asked him.

'What lorry?' he growled, after a moment of interpretative silence. It was the growl of something wounded that had been disturbed in its refuge.

⌒

The only time I can remember my father showing me any physical affection during the later part of my childhood was when I told him I wanted to be a priest. I must have been about eleven or twelve; time to begin thinking seriously about secondary school and the future. We were sitting up together in bed. I don't know how he got to be in the same bed as me, but it wouldn't have been very unusual in those days. In my memory, he is on the inside of the bed: perhaps he had invited me into it that morning for a serious chat about what I wanted to be in life. In any case, when I told him I wanted to be a priest, he put his arm around my shoulders and brought me as close to him as his distance would permit; our shoulders touched for a while.

'It's what I have always prayed for,' he said.

I remember that I burst into tears: perhaps because my father was showing me some belated affection or because of the prospect of renouncing the world; or perhaps for both reasons, considering the way my father's affection seemed to be tied in with my becoming a priest.

⌐

Mrs Feehan got into an awful lather about God. He was everywhere and if you hid even in the very centre of the biggest mountain to commit sin, he would see you. He sees everything you do. God was like my father: I couldn't get away from him.

Mrs Feehan tortured herself more than she tortured us about God. It was an awesome spectacle, a strange entertainment, to watch as she worked herself up and the spittle began to appear on her lips. She went into a frenzy about the sufferings of Christ, but rarely visited them on us. Occasionally she caned us across the palm of the hand, almost gently, for some boldness or other. She would wince as the cane made contact: it could truly be said, in her particular case, that the punishment hurt the giver as much as it hurt the receiver.

I am sorry to have to say that the visiting of the sufferings of Christ on us was largely my father's department. He was the one to make Christian Soldiers of us. Mrs Feehan's pantomime of the Scourging at the Pillar, when she brought a boy out in front of the class and laid her cane on his back to show us the angle at which the thongs had fallen on Jesus, was a dumb show of what came later, in the higher classes taught by my father.

⤳

The clink of cruets in the silence. The long spoon, like a cook's long ladle in miniature, standing out of the water cruet. The priest comes over to the side of the altar where I am standing with the two cruets in my hands, the miniature towel resting, waiter-like, over my wrist. He takes the tiny ladle and drops one drop from it into the chalice of wine, to signify the water that flowed out of Christ's side with the plenteous blood when Longinus pierced him with a spear (just in case he wasn't dead yet after those three hours of agony).

Oh the tinkle of the cruets in the silence! In those days I loved serving mass: 'Sure it's my only hobby in the mornings', I remember once saying to myself, contentedly, on my way to the friary chapel.

Sometimes now, lying on my bed in the middle of the

night and listening to downpours, I think of the rain as my father's temper, how it raged, then lulled, then raged again, all the worse, with thunder and lightning, inexhaustible as his frustration. And comparing my father's temper to the rain tells me two things: one, that it was a force of nature, frightening, flood-making; and two, that it was great and terrible to me as a child, and the fear of it has been impressed indelibly on my mind.

And I think of how I have had to enter into a post-Christian era to write my story. I have had to step outside the religion of my childhood to get some perspective on the people who taught children about the love of God, and how they could have been the same people who afflicted them with the sufferings of Christ.

And I sometimes wonder whether the so-called Christian centuries were really Christian at all. Were they not rather an epoch in which genuine religious sentiment was exploited for the maintenance of social order?

These are the kinds of thoughts that come to me when I lie awake at night, listening to my father's temper in the rain.

↜

There are times when I wake early in such a rage that I cannot stay in bed. I have to go downstairs and act out my wave-therapy without the benefit of waves, in dumb show so as not to wake my wife and son, gesturing obscenely, silently mouthing the most lurid blasphemies against God, my father-God, my father who acted as if he was God, my father who, to my most bitter disappointment, turned out to be anyone but God.

Occasionally I act out a mock-religious ritual. I take out a photograph and place it on my desk, the altar of my imprecations, standing it against the word processor. The photograph shows my father in the role of Master, the cane in his hand pointing out the words of *Faith of Our Fathers* on the blackboard of some school where he taught in later years:

> Faith of our fathers, living still
> In spite of dungeon, fire and sword …

And I know in my blind fury that, despite a certain portrait dignity, there is a grey snail-slime all over his face, the grey snail-slime of an alien breaking through the fake human skin. Mockingly, I genuflect in front of the grey snail-slime creature who thought he was an infallible god, impossible to contradict, who knew everything and even if you told him something he didn't know, he'd tell it back to you the next week in the patriarchal manner of imparting information to an ignorant offspring.

And all hail to the Almighty Cane! The cane that slaps and spanks when it is not pointing out the words of *Faith of Our Fathers*. Or else it points to a cylinder whose volume must be measured, 'the Volume' becoming a child's jokey nickname which hides the true nature of the event that gave rise to it, a leathering that marked him for life.

Ah but we mustn't forget, sure we mustn't, the other persons in this unholy trinity? Oh faith and begob we mustn't: when we pay our homage to the Cane, we mustn't forget the Flat of the Hand and the Fist. And so to end our devotions appropriately, we make, as we always do, the Sign of the Cross, the Sign of the Awful Crossness: in the name of the Fist, and of the Cane, and of the Flat of the Hand, Amen.

Old Snail-Face. Old Fog-Face. Old Fuck-Face.

I put the photograph back in its box and go to the kitchen to make a cup of coffee. I am frightened by the power of the anger that has spiralled into my head. Is this really the Little Boy Who Never Said A Word, speaking out at last in a temper as fierce as his father's? Or is it someone new and hateful and aggressive, who says worse things now because the little boy didn't say anything then? And is this the way monsters are born out of nice and quiet and remote children the world over?

'I'm taking that on board, Ciaran,' says my new therapist. 'I think it's none other than the little boy. But that's all right.'

⤆

Instead of the religion of my childhood, I now have the Almighty Therapist. He, too, can be a kind of god, a dogmatic know-all. My first therapist was too like my father to be of any use to me, because he expected me to play, in relation to his wisdom, the kind of inert, receptive role I need to subvert in myself. But my main reason for dispensing with him was that he jumped to theory-bound conclusions about sexual abuse without waiting for the evidence. I have enough negative things to say about my father without resorting to false memories.

All around me where I now live, the religion of my childhood is still alive and vibrant. I am surrounded by churches and Catholic schools: when I look out a window in the morning, I can see statues of saints, patriarchs and prophets at roof-level on nearby buildings, as if my house had been transported overnight to the centre of St Peter's Square. In summer a Solemn Novena causes traffic jams for over a week around a church just down the road, and the cars have back-window stickers bearing the words *Solemn Novena* and the dates of its duration alongside the more usual declarations of support for Manchester United, Liverpool, or a local hurling team. In the Small Ads pages of local newspapers, devout people still insert prayers for the benefit of others: *Prayer to the Virgin Mary Never Known to Fail; Prayer to St Jude the Patron of Hopeless Cases.* Sometimes the thought occurs to me that I might be better off cutting out one of these prayers and reciting it daily than having recourse to another therapist.

My new therapist, however, has soft eyes, much softer than those of my former one, more receptive. Eyes that not only beam out energy, but receive it in. He, too, has a problem about the way I see my life prospects (that I will struggle on, and then die), but he actually says so. Then he goes on to suggest – merely suggest – some kind of positive change in my personality as an alternative possibility that I might entertain, a different map of my life to browse over for a few weeks.

I tell him that I am fed up of my hostile feelings; that they're not doing me any good.

'I hear what you're saying, Ciaran, but there's a difference between expressing hostile feelings and having a generally hostile attitude. If you don't learn to express the feelings, you'll go around exuding a kind of hostile aura. The problem with feelings is they're so bound up together: if you can't express hostile ones, very often the positive ones don't come to the surface either. A ferocious row is often followed by an intensely loving reconciliation. I sense that this is your big fear, Ciaran: you're afraid of your anger, you keep it down, but it presses out and spreads all over your personality to create bad vibes.

'Take the example we've just been discussing. You feel that shop assistants ignore you. Can I perhaps put it to you that they sense your negative aura? People *do* sense these things. And you *do* exude a negative sort of energy; it was the first thing I noticed about you. When you first came to me, I had a strong sense of the attitude of the hurt child: that the whole world should be at his beck and call, to compensate for what happened to him. And if it isn't at your beck and call, then it's to be condemned: the shop assistant who ignores you and goes to arrange the shelves, the therapist who doesn't come up with an instant solution.

'I think we need to work on this, Ciaran. Getting rid of that aura, expressing your feelings in a meaningful way. The next time you go into a shop and the assistant ignores you, why don't you just say *Excuse me, can I be served?* In a pleasant *but assertive* manner, rather than just standing there, fuming? Think of it as a game if you like. Give yourself points for attracting their attention. And eye-contact, Ciaran. Look them in the eyes…'

My new therapist also holds strongly to the view that I must be the one to unearth any memories of sexual abuse by my father, and he is extremely wary of false memories.

'But what about my dream?' I ask.

'Dreams are difficult, Ciaran. That dream of having sex with your father doesn't mean you *have had* sex with your father – any more than a dream of flying means you have actually flown. I'm taking that dream very much on board, though I haven't heard enough from you yet; I don't hear where it's coming from. But you do need to be aware that dreams are very jumbled. I might tentatively suggest that this dream is a classic example of *condensation*. There's the wish to be united with your father, and there's something else, some wish about your sex life, perhaps: we still haven't touched on that subject. The two elements have been locked together in the seemingly irrational logic of your unconscious. I'm not saying that dreams don't ever unearth buried memories, but they generally work in a different way...'

⟿

Dream of last night. There is a place on high, up a wide flight of steps. I am afraid to go up, but my nine-year-old son urges me on. The place turns out to be a monastery; there are white-robed figures like Cistercians playing billiards on a balcony. One of them lifts his head briefly from his billiard cue to say that he knows from the look of me that I'm going through an awful time. He advises me to diversify my sex-life. He particularly recommends oral sex. The point is that if I want to be happier, I should get more into sex. I am grateful and relieved that someone has noticed my plight, and I thank him warmly. He nods, and continues playing billiards, as if the whole business was an everyday occurrence.

7

Words and music

I have a recurrent dream that I
am drowning and my father's life is being replayed before
my eyes. But it's not the conventional kind of dream that
occurs in sleep; it's not even a waking dream: it's a reality-
dream. The people I have trusted enough to tell them
about the kind of childhood I had are usually more interested in my father than in me. Inevitably, some kind of
vague sketch of my father begins to emerge when I talk
about my young self, and the listener, not knowing any
longer how to relate to the half-formed world of childhood, seems to prefer the solidity of an adult life, an interesting one at that, a fit subject maybe for a Greek tragedy,
certainly for a novel.

My father's is the story of a man torn by his own
internal contradictions and the post-colonial and other
contradictions of his society: an artist who could not
imagine himself without a permanent pensionable job in
the public service of a recently independent state, firstly
because the public service was his mother's definition of

reality for him, and secondly because he very quickly found himself (unlike the famous painter) lumbered with a good Catholic uncontracepted family of six; a photographer aspiring to publish his glamour snapshots in British magazines, who was simultaneously a teacher lecturing his female pupils about the dangers of vanity, lipstick and 'silly notions'; a fervent nationalist and promoter of the Irish language, whose own father was a sailor in the British Navy and had taught him as a boy to say *Down with the rebels!* at a time when the whole country was converting to the rebels' cause; the child of a largely absent father who suddenly left him forever by dying of TB ...

And so on and so forth, as my father used always to say when he was temporarily stuck for words, to convey the impression that the argument was endless, the complications multiple, the unsaid of equal importance, but of far greater length, than the said. And so on and so forth, and I am knocked down by a sudden wave of pity, again in danger of drowning, with my father's life ready to unfold before my eyes. And the only remedy is to scramble to my feet and swear at the next wave from the height of my anger, ignoring the lifeguard, the censor.

Here is a tricky passage to be navigated, and I am deafened by shouts of dry-land sailors guiding me towards the rocks: *tell us more about your father.* The ghost that raves at memory's window cannot tolerate this. He has climbed out of the window and entered my body; he has taken over the steering, he guides my fingers on the keys of the word processor. And rightly so: how ironic it would be if, setting out to write about how my personality was overwhelmed by my father's as a child, I should end up writing a memoir in which he was the dominant figure.

For God's sake, don't bother with him types the ghost.

I now know a lot more about my father than I did as a child. I have enough information to write another book; there is, as the psychiatrist said about Basil Fawlty, 'material for an entire conference'. But the only relevant material for present purposes is what I knew of my father when I was a child; how he appeared to me then. The centre-stage is already cluttered: it is dominated by my ghost and my shadow-self, and the now-grave, now-frenetic dance they (we) perform in an effort to merge and become a person of substance.

> She stepped out and he stepped in again;
> he stepped out and she stepped in again …

Let's have some more words and music.

⤺

My first music lesson was *doh ray me, doh ray me, doh ray me fah me ray doh: Here we go, sure and slow, up and down and in a row.*

The music teacher was a rotund shiny-faced man, dressed in suit and waistcoat. Generally good-humoured and full of dry jokes, he could suddenly take an irascible turn. Sometimes when I played a wrong note, he'd rap me on the knuckles with a short cane that tapered to a point, which he wielded as a conductor's baton.

He was middle-aged and unmarried and lived with his mother in a house furnished with 'the relics of ould dacency': fusty-smelling embroidered curtains and drapes, sofas, Regency-type chairs, a grand piano. His mother was rarely seen: I pictured her living upstairs, in an identical room.

You walked from the hall through the gloomy parlour to a small room at the back which looked out on the garden. In this room was another piano, an ordinary one, and a chair with a round seat that spun up or down to adjust to your height. Against the opposite wall there was a bench, where the next pupil, if she arrived early, could sit and wait while you were being put through the ear-test, always the last item of the lesson.

The music teacher sat in an armchair beside the piano and made jokes, his cane within reach of your knuckles or backside. He always began the lesson by announcing, *We're off, we're off, on a soft and level country road, no stones to hurt the horse's feet.*

I also went to the music teacher to learn the Latin for serving mass.

— *Introibo ad altare Dei.*
— *Ad Deum qui laetificat iuventutem meum.*

I was intrigued by the presence of a cat in the middle of the first response in the Latin Mass. What could a cat be doing in the middle of this sacred incomprehensible chant?

The music teacher had a stock of jokey mnemonics to aid us in learning the Latin:

— *Dominus vobiscum.*
— *Et cum spiritu tuo.*

This antiphon and response translated as:

— Dominick, did the biscuits come?
— Yes, and the spirits too.

I loved the sounds, the strange unintelligible music, the broad dark vowels of Church Latin, and often muttered the responses to myself on the way to or from serving Mass:

Quia tu es Deus, quare me repulisti, et quare
tristis incedo, dum affligit me inimicus?

That was a beautiful response altogether, not a cat in it or anything concrete at all, just an ordering of haunting sounds that opened casements on the perilous foam of another world. It was like the poem by Keats that my father once recited to us in class:

Season of mists and mellow fruitfulness,
Close bosom-friend of the maturing sun...

When I heard 'To Autumn' for the first time, I understood almost as little of it as I understood of the Latin Mass. But here too I was fascinated by the sounds, their ripe slow-moving opacity.

⌒

I didn't know what to make of the music teacher feeling my thigh and kissing me on the lips. He always had to have a kiss before I left, and some days he wanted a lot of kisses, and not only when I was leaving. And other days he put his hand further up my thigh than usual and jiggled around with my private parts. These were just things that the music teacher did, so I didn't pay much attention to them, and anyway on the days when he kissed me and felt my thigh a lot, he didn't whack me, so I just got on with the lesson until it was over and as soon as I was out on the street, I forgot all about it until the next time.

Recently, I had a dream of climbing a spiral stairs in a tower, and finding my music teacher, with some shadowy henchmen, in a big high-ceilinged room at the top. He is a mad scientist, conducting experiments of some kind. He says: *When the high winds blow, all kinds of things happen here.* The wind begins to blow strongly, and various machines and wires and pulleys start swirling around and jerking forwards and backwards on the ceiling and high up on the walls. Out of all this commotion, a single chocolate wrapped in coloured silver-foil flies down and lands on my lap. I take the wrapper off and eat the chocolate.

It was rumoured around the town that the music teacher was a *younik*, which meant he had no balls and was generally harmless.

> Hitler had only one big ball,
> Goering had two but they were small,
> Himmler had something sim'lar,
> But poor old Go-balls had no balls at all.

The music teacher was like Go-balls: he had no balls at all.

⤸

I had a great capacity for remembering irreverent jingles. I heard many of these jingles from other altar boys in the friary or from the big boys up at the Horgans or from my black-sheep brother.

> Moll and Ducker sat under a bush.
> Moll let a fart, and Ducker said *Hush!*

This couplet referred to an old man and woman in dire poverty, Moll and Ducker Bailey, who lived in a hovel on the edge of town. They never washed their clothes and had bad smells. Moll's smell was worse than Ducker's, but Ducker's clothes were dirtier than Moll's. There was an impasto of decades of grease on Ducker's coat and trousers, which gave them a swamplike sheen. Moll was reputed to be walking with fleas, and was nicknamed 'Fleaballs': in this ultimate insult lay the suggestion that she was so filthy and hairy, she couldn't really be feminine.

I often wondered whether Moll and Ducker weren't angels in disguise, but really they stayed around the town too long. Angels just appeared out of nowhere and went back there; they didn't have a history. And another thing: angels would hardly even *know* the kind of language Moll used when children called her names.

> Hail Mary full of grace,
> Ducker Bailey won the race.

121

Holy Mary Mother of God,
Going to school is all a cod.

And why wouldn't going to school be all a cod, when your
father, the Master, is there, belting you from one end of the
classroom to the other?

Down in the valley where nobody knows,
I met Betty Grable without any clothes.
I gave her a shilling if she was willing,
I gave her a crown if she'd lie down.
I gave her a nick if she'd take off her slip,
And out jumped me ould black jack.

One day, I announced this piece of doggerel to my
mother in the parlour. She was so shocked, she immediately called in my father and made me repeat it in front of
him. Surprisingly (again), he took a lenient view. Perhaps
he was trying to hide his amusement. Perhaps he wanted to
contradict my mother. He insisted that I didn't know the
meaning of what I was saying, and of course he was right. I
was bewildered by the episode. I had probably wanted to
impress my mother, to show how good I was at learning
things by heart, as I had previously impressed my uncle
with a recitation of 'Kelly the Boy from Killane'. I knew that
'black jack' was a liquorice-flavoured toffee-bar; and I was
sure that Betty Grable had been given a piece of toffee at
the end of the verse for doing everything she was told.

Poulacapall: the Horse's Hole. My first brother used to make jokes about that. 'How would you like to live in a horse's hole?'

Inistioge: In-a-steak. My uncle used to go fishing to In-a-steak, and come back with a basketful of brown trout. It was funny that you could get so many fish in a town that sounded like meat, because meat was the opposite to fish. You could eat meat six days of the week, but on Friday you had to eat fish, for penance. That was because fish wasn't supposed to taste nice. But even white fish could taste very nice if it was served with a white sauce. Was it cheating to serve fish on Friday with a white sauce which made it taste good? Was Granny-in-Cork, my father's mother, committing a sin because her Friday fish was so delicious?

It was all right to eat brown trout on a Friday, because it had hardly any taste at all, except for the skin, when it was fried. Was it a sin to eat the skin on a Friday? My aunt didn't want me to eat the skin, but she didn't say it was a sin; she just said it was bad for me. The skin was for the cat. It wasn't fair that the cat, which was only an animal, got the best bit.

Friday: Fry-day. Funny that you weren't allowed to eat meat on a Friday, because meat was mostly fried, and you'd imagine that Fry-day would be the day for all kinds of fried stuff. But most people simply boiled a bit of whiting in water and ate it without any sauce, and that really was penance.

Sometimes they ate a bit of cod. A bit of a cod. If you told the parish priest you ate meat on a Friday, he'd roar you out of the confession box. *He* didn't think Friday was a bit of a cod.

Words clung in my memory the way sticklebacks clung to my pullover. Rows of words, patterns of words, like the stealthy collage of sticklebacks the boy in the desk behind me arranged on my back. The sticklebacks are long since gone, but the words remain.

> Brian Boru, the King of Munster,
> Let a fart and knocked a youngster.
> The youngster said he'd tell his mother.
> 'If you do, I'll let another.'

> Janey Mack me shirt is black,
> What will I do on Sunday?
> Go to bed and cover me head
> And not get up till Monday.

Hostile words were more full of terror than hostile reality. The reality came and went but the words would not go away. *I'll beat you into the middle of next week.* The threat, when the action was suspended, grew in the vividness of my imagination. Nothing was worse than suspended terror: I was an anxious child.

The Irish Catholic's prediction of Three Dark Days for 1960, when the powers of evil would be loosed on the world, occasionally held me in a mental paralysis. Every so often, the prophecy fell across my young life, a shadow that remained for hours before lifting just as suddenly. I would wake thinking of the Three Dark Days, and of the necessity of praying that the world might be spared them. I was regularly visited by such phantoms. God, of course, would eventually exorcise all these ghouls and goblins by the sheer light and love of his arrival; but it seemed that he had to be constantly implored, that I had to be always on my knees, or else the powers of wickedness would have their way. As if it was necessary to reach a critical mass of prayer before God would arrive.

Parcels of American comics were sent to us by our cousins. Some of these, too, were full of terrors. I remember a story called 'The Jaws of the Creeping Death'. There was an enormous set of moving teeth which devoured everything in its path, and words in the speech-bubble above a doomed woman's head: *It's coming closer! Its jaws are opening! It ... Oooh no!*

⌐

While I was still staying overnight at my maternal grandmother's, I graduated from reading nothing but comics to reading occasional books. I received books as presents. *Grimm's Fairy Tales* was one of the first, given to me by my uncle. I was horrified by some of these stories. I remember one which involved the hero in a ritual of fear in a haunted castle. He had to stay in the castle for three nights, to be accosted at midnight on the first two nights by hellish creatures, who would attack and terrify him till dawn, and leave him half-mad and half-dead. If he endured this ordeal, at midnight on the third night the hero's body and mind would be healed, and he'd become owner of the exorcized castle and marry the princess. I imagined the solicitor's house as the haunted castle: it was the biggest house I knew, and it had a wide staircase. The hero was waiting upstairs in the big bedroom. The clock was striking midnight and he could hear the stealthy footsteps on the stairs of the demons who were coming to torment him.

There was another story about a boy who was granted the power of wishing, of having his wishes come true. This boy had it so good, I was quickly in his shoes. I was no longer just a boy who wished, but the one who had the *power*. I wished for mundane things like Kimberley biscuits, a No. 12 Meccano Set (the solicitor's son had one, whereas I had only a No. 0 and a No. 0a). I wished I was living in a big house like the solicitor's, with a swimming pool. I wished for extraordinary things, like being able to fly and instant travel and changing water into lemonade. But the individual wishes weren't important. This gift wasn't just a case of having a finite number of wishes come true, as in some fairy tales; it wasn't a genie in a lamp which could be stolen; this was the permanent power of realizing anything at all you wanted at any given moment. And if what you wanted had awkward consequences, another wish could undo them. As the boy with the power of wishing, I had omnipotent desires. And I could afford to use them for other people as well as for myself. Above all, I could use them to be admired, to be loved.

When I wasn't the boy with the wishing power, I was Batman's friend, Robin the Boy Wonder. There was something pre-erotic or proto-erotic about this: Robin the Boy Wonder wore a kind of leotard that revealed the shapes of his legs right up to the tops of his thighs. But besides showing off his legs, the shapely hero also carried out all sorts of brave deeds, protecting the public from evil conspiracies.

Later I became Michael Rodgers. He was a boy of my own age and invention who helped detectives to catch criminals. He wore ordinary clothes, nothing fancy; the one important detail was his long trousers. I didn't wear long trousers until the day of my Confirmation, when I was eleven, but Michael Rodgers had them at the age of nine.

Michael Rodgers was an expert at jumping on the running boards of cars. He would run down the main street of my home town, gun in hand, chasing a getaway van. When he came up level with some local car that happened to have a running board, he'd jump on and tell the driver 'Follow that van!' People going about their business on the pavements would stop to admire him.

'There goes Michael Rodgers again,' they'd say. 'Where would we be without him?'

After the Sunday Matinee, we'd spill out the doors of the cinema on to the wide pavement, galloping on imaginary horses, shooting at one another, shouting 'Yippee! Yi-hee!' If you were shot, you had to count up to sixty before you could come alive again. If you were shot six times, you were really dead; you were out of the game. We argued and fought about whose turn it was to be Roy Rodgers. He was, after all, King of the Cowboys. But one day my first brother declared that he was going to be Hopalong Cassidy *all the time*; no one else could ever be Hopalong Cassidy again. As a guarantee of his right to be Hopalong Cassidy, Anthony was wearing the Hopalong Cassidy suit sent by our American cousins, because by this time it had been passed down from me to him.

After Anthony's declaration, we all adopted a no-change policy and the other heroes were distributed: I became Roy Rodgers, someone else became Alan Ladd, others became the Lone Ranger and Gene Autry. Because of my curly hair, a wit from the Burma Road suggested that it might be better to call me Fuzzy Knight.

～

I've met some folks who say that I'm a dreamer,
And I've no doubt there's truth in what they say.
But sure a body's bound to be a dreamer
When all the things he loves are far away.

My father's favourite song: he sang it all through my childhood. His singing it signalled a calmer mood, an onset of tranquillity. One of the activities that calmed him was rearranging books; transferring them from one cupboard to another, from one set of shelves to another, putting them in a more classified order. He bought an enormous amount of books, although he read very few of them. To this day, one of my mother's greatest resentments is the amount of money he spent on books. *I wouldn't mind if he read any of them*, she says to me. Now that he's dead, she's given most of them away to her children, and as a result I'm the possessor of several first editions which may be, for all I know, of considerable value. The only problem is that, in his possessiveness, he has stamped each book over and over, on various pages, with a rubber stamp bearing his name and address. This defacement will no doubt take from their value.

My father spent much more time rearranging his books than reading them. Entire afternoons were devoted to the task, and as he rearranged, he sang. He was a good singer, and had a large repertoire of songs; many of them were *Sean Nós*, such as *Táimse im' Chodladh* and *Bog Braon do'n tSeanduine*, but he'd intersperse these with 1950s' hits by Ruby Murray and Vera Lynn; and of course, with *The Isle of Inisfree.*

> And when the moonlight creeps across the rooftops
> Of this great city, wondrous though it be,
> I scarcely feel its music or its laughter,
> I'm once again back home in Inisfree.

All through my childhood, my real father was there on the shelves, congealed in books; *reified,* as the philosophers say. He was available only as a memorial to what might have been: a commemorative library, a museum of volumes on the visual arts, painting, literature and music. These were the things my father considered to be really important in life, but lacking the courage or the opportunity of his convictions, he had to be content with a monument to unrealized potential. And he was at peace and sang among his books because he was communing with his real self.

As a teenager, when I discovered my own interest in art, and particularly in literature, by spending hours in my father's museum of broken dreams, he would suddenly appear at my shoulder with advice on how to spend my time there. Once he said, 'You must read Chekhov. He is regarded as the greatest short-story writer ever.' Another time he told me that if I wanted my stories to be published, I should put a *twist* in them, after the manner of O. Henry. And one day he explained the Impressionists to me: 'To see what's in their paintings, you have to stand well back from them.'

My father: the curator of a museum in honour of a man who might have been, a man I could have loved.

> And precious things are dreams unto an exile;
> They take him o'er the land across the sea.
> Especially when it happens he's an exile
> From that dear lovely Isle of Inisfree.

⌐

I remember my father bringing me for a haircut to the barber's next door to our shop; I think we were both getting haircuts, father and son. My father's hearty laugh in the barber's shop. Jokes about hair and baldness and quiffs and Brylcreem.

I was his son then, because he laughed at my quick response to his tease about my curls and how, seeing that they were gone, the girls wouldn't look at me any more. *That's what you think!* I said, a reply taken straight from *The Beano*. My father's approving laughter behind me, as I made my exit, heading towards my grandmother's under the winter glow of streetlamps. My father had laughed at my joke. When I reached the end of the town, I ran happily, with light and the promise of light.

Much much later, when we were living in Dublin, and

my father had been outmanoeuvred for some important position in the Gaelic League and had retired from his *cumann*, he frequently sang a song of treachery, of being given poisoned chickens to eat on golden plates:

D'itheas sicíní nimhe ar phláitíní óir,
Agus cóirigh mo leaba, táim breoite go leor …

He still had a hearty laugh, but sadly he no longer laughed at reality, at his son's duff jokes or Sadie Kenneally's innu-endos, only at the box in the corner of the living room, at the canned antics of the Three Stooges.

A couple of years ago I heard a poet read a poem about role-reversal: how he felt that he was now the father, his father the son. Sometimes I feel like I'm giving birth to my father.

What happened you, Dad? How did the light of your laugh in the barber's shop suddenly darken to the snarl of an animal?

Walking by the sea at Spanish Point, I sense the dis-persed presence of my father, the father I never really knew, who was, like the sea, emotionally dumb, and has now entered into a deeper level of dumbness, speaking the language of silence and disintegration. Particles of his body are molecules of ozone; other particles have entered the more complex structures of kelp and seaweed; some have even inveigled their way into the digestive tracts of cormorants and sandpipers. His soul is dispersed and diluted in the air, in the look of the water and the look of the land. At last the man who never admitted to a fault in his lifetime, who was *stubborn to a fault*, is truly humble, so humble that he is nothing and speaks powerfully. He explains how all those letters he sent me, full of redundant advice, enclosing advertisements from newspapers for permanent pensionable full-time posts, were really the inappropriate utterances of a person to whom the expression of fatherly affection was a foreign language.

8

The toughening

When I was recalled from my posting at my grandmother's, at about the age of nine or ten, I had to endure with the others the trials of being cooped up in a small back yard every weekday after dinner. My solitude was severely dented. My mother tells me I used come out to the shop with my hands covering my ears, complaining: 'The noise! The noise!' The back yard was a place of survival of the fittest.

We often got a tuppenny wafer after dinner. Anthony devised a sort of 'South Sea Bubble', and the rest of us were invited to invest in it. The investment was half your ice cream every day for six or seven weeks, and the promised return at the end of that period was a train set or, in my sister's case, a doll. There was no knowing where these handsome dividends were going to come from, but those who didn't buy into the scheme were subjected to the 'Tee dee Mun'.

The 'Tee dee Mun' was a ritual chant which heralded physical assault. Anthony chanted it to the air of the BBC's signature tune for 'Music While You Work': *Tee dee Mun, dee Mun Mun Tee dee Mun* … As he chanted, he raised his right hand slowly. The thumb and index finger were joined to form a circle, the way someone tasting a sauce would do it to signal perfection. As the chant came to a climax, he would bring his hand down suddenly on the recusant investor, pinching him on the shoulder or the back of the neck.

As the eldest, I had a position of responsibility in the back yard, one that I didn't always live up to. Anthony rarely threatened me, and I often intervened to prevent him from bullying the younger ones. But I, too, eventually became an ice-cream speculator, though my powers of persuasion derived from abuse of the respect in which I was held, rather than from the threat of physical force.

We developed an entire culture in the back yard. There were rituals of homage and appeasement. There were mythologies: the Kurdi-Yana and the Vatsin-Yana were two monsters who visited the back yard after dark, and woe betide any child who was in the toilet-hut when they came. We had peculiar sayings like 'I'm as sick as *two* dogs'.

We were close to evolving an entire language. Anthony kept pigeons in coops with lettuce-wire fronts: the pigeons were called 'laerspas'. A rough sensation on the skin was a 'ratchy' feeling. Sensations could be 'ratchy hot' or 'ratchy cold'. If we weren't sure how to make an adjective of a noun, we added the ending -*rilly*: 'I'd love a pound-rilly ice cream.' We also had our own way of making abstract nouns from adjectives: 'Look at the *thinth* of her', meaning her thinness.

'A-chi' was a term of mockery connoting a failed attempt to perform something for our collective amusement. This term came into being when our youngest, John Daniel, under orders from Anthony, attempted to ad-lib a comic act. He got stage fright and all that came from his mouth was 'A-chi, a-chi'. But John Daniel's stage-death caused more amusement than all the successful turns put together.

'Ne fulanti lagooze' was the command to improvise one of these amusing sequences:

> Ne fulanti lagooze:
> come over here, Tipsy, and make me amused.

Everyone had a nickname. There were definitely six of us now: Gik, Volume, Nyiffy, Miss Madam Climber, Dargle and Fag. My sister tried to climb the back-yard wall once and fell off. My mother's unsympathetic response was 'Well, if it isn't Miss Madam Climber'. 'Fag' had something to do with cigarettes, I think; but John Daniel, the smallest and most put-upon, had a full official title which was very long indeed: *the Fag Hag Jackaboody Jahyal Tipsy (or Titsy) May Hay Jay and Take Your Time Poking the Fire*. The last bit, about poking the fire, arose from a time when he had asked my mother for money to go to the pictures. 'And take your time poking the fire,' he added diplomatically; in other words, no need to break your neck rushing to the till before you've got the fire going properly. My name, Gik, stemmed from my first babyish attempts to pronounce my real name. Sometimes I was backhandedly honoured by the addition of the definite article: 'Here comes the Gik.' Whenever I laid down the law, preventing someone from carrying out his desires, I was 'Big Gik': 'Big Gik won't let us do anything.'

'Dargle' was a playful variation of Darcy. 'Nyiffy' origin-ated in a speech mannerism: the brother of mine who had to endure this nickname often prefaced his pronounce-ments with the sound 'nyiff'. In mockery, Anthony extended the name to 'Nyiffy Daw Tex Daw': with stronger stresses on the two 'Daws', this was a truly grating sound. It is per-haps coincidental that in the parlance of my home town (as elsewhere) a 'daw' was a simpleton or idiot.

Thrown together without escape in the back yard, we had constant fights and quarrels. But there was also a kind of oppressed companionship: we were the *compañeros* of a muddled liberation army.

⌐

It was a rude awakening, moving back from my grand-mother's to my parents' house. I arrived with boxes full of toys and American comics. These *Dell* comics were in great demand at the time; much more sought-after than British comics. The American ones were always in full colour, whereas even the most popular British ones, such as *The Beano* and *The Dandy,* had many strips in black and white, and some were entirely black and white apart from their covers, which promised what the insides did not deliver. Another factor which set the American comics apart from the British ones was their pleasant smell, a kind of perfume you could enjoy by putting your nose to a page.

Comics weren't just read; they were possessed. Handling them, feeling the silkiness of the covers, smelling the aroma of the inside pages, were acts of possession, of possessiveness. We lovingly arranged our stocks in their cardboard boxes, the way my father rearranged his books on the shelves.

Swapping comics was a brisk trade in our town, and Anthony was at the very centre of it. He negotiated the difficult terrain between the comics of the children of Main Street's petty bourgeoisie and the comics of the Burma Road. He was a middle-man who, when he was 'done' by a dealer from the Burma Road, passed off the inferior goods to one of us or one of our neighbours. I suspect that he received favours (such as cigarettes) for moving petty-bourgeois stock into the council estate, altering the balance of comic-wealth in favour of the less privileged.

These transactions were frequently accomplished with the aid of force or threat. Bigger boys intimidated smaller boys into parting with their superior comics. As an altar boy, for a period I lived in fear of going to serve at the evening devotions because I had refused to swap comics with a boy who lived near the friary, and he had threatened revenge. One evening after benediction, I spotted him waiting outside the friary gates. I asked an older altar boy for protection. The older boy threatened this minor thug with the police and, as far as I can remember, it was enough to end the harassment.

Within twenty-four hours of my arrival back home from my grandmother's, Anthony had stripped me of most of my childhood wealth. Fooled by his sales pitch, I had swapped my collection of Dinkies for dubious models that turned out to have wonky wheels and other defects. I had swapped twelve of my best Dell comics for some bumper issue that, as I soon discovered, had several pages missing.

⌒

A great change came over my eating habits when I returned home. My supper was no longer secure, my right to it no longer uncontested. Even though I had always eaten dinner at home on weekdays after school, I remained detached from that particular scramble during the years I was staying in my grandmother's: if I lost out at dinner, I could compensate at supper, and in a leisurely way, dreaming or reading as I ate. But now, at all meals, I was one pig among six.

At suppertime, Barbara put a breadboard heaped with buttered slices of bread in the middle of the table, and the six of us sat around, grabbing and eating as quickly as we could. Each of us had a mug of tea as well, but we hardly dared to take a drink from it until we had finished eating.

At dinner, when food was given to us on separate plates, Anthony would finish first and harass the rest of us by pushing his empty plate around the table, bringing it to a halt alongside one of ours with a clunk, and demanding *Any cattle for my cattle truck?* Those who refused to give him a bit of meat or a potato were either bullied or blackmailed, depending on their age.

Anthony always managed to have something on me, some secret information that would be embarrassing to me if it was made public. When I was about eleven, I kept a diary, in which I entered vows and resolutions. One of these entries was a promise to God that I would do my utmost to remain in a state of holy purity. Anthony had got his hands on the diary, and if I refused him food at dinner, he'd raise his eyes to heaven in mock sanctity and say *Holy Purity! Holy Purity!* I usually resisted the blackmail, but it sometimes led to a tussle, the upsetting of plates of mutton stew, carrots and potatoes mushed into the floor, and punishment from Barbara.

⌣

The Goog was our chauffeur. He was a small swarthy man from the New Houses. He probably got his name from the fact that he always referred to an egg as a 'guggie', and then the second syllable was cut off, the first syllable lengthened and the definite article added, in deference to the fact that he was a bit of a character: 'He comes the Goog'.

He was not a permanent chauffeur in a uniform, but a part-time, spasmodic one. Sometimes my father went to the Royal Imperial Hotel in the city for unknown reasons, and it was the Goog who drove him there. Perhaps my father hired the Goog for his trips to the city because he foresaw the possibility that he would drink. But more often than not, the Goog was the one who got drunk, and my father had to drive home. My father would then swear never to hire the Goog again; but a few weeks later, some new contingency saw our spasmodic chauffeur once more behind the wheel.

One evening my father broke his elbow in the back yard. He was standing on a rickety chair, camera to eye, trying to get the right angle on some subject. A leg of the chair gave way. He told us afterwards that his first thought was to save the camera: that was why he had landed on his elbow.

My father would have nothing to do with doctors or hospitals. *Stay away from them,* he used to say. *They'll kill you in the end.* Instead, he insisted on going to a bonesetter, who lived on the top of a mountain somewhere in Laois or Offaly. The Goog was hired to drive him there. They were away for most of the night.

My father was childishly proud of the fact that he had broken his elbow not just in one, but in three places. For the rest of his life, he took every opportunity to mention the fact. But the bonesetter, for all my father's faith in him and distrust of hospitals, did not do a very good job. Ever afterwards, my father's elbow described a wide sweeping arc whenever he lifted a piece of bread or a spoonful of egg to his mouth.

The Goog was a spasmodic man, not only in his capacity as chauffeur, but also by temperament. He was prone to sudden unaccountable spasms of hilarity. Whenever one of these fits seized him, he would reach for the peaked cap which he wore down over his eyes, grip it in a strangler's clench and then fling it at the object of his amusement, which was often my father. Once when we were leaving for our summer holiday in West Cork, he flung it at our departing Morris Eight. Perhaps, in those strange times, it was an expression of affection.

For months afterwards, when we were sullen and gloomy in the back yard, one of us, face brightening unaccountably, vacuously, would announce *The Goog threw his hat at the car!* And we would all laugh insanely, because in our misery we had identified with the Goog's capacity for sudden lunatic mirth, and it needed only the words which embodied the memory to release us into a spasm of inane hilarity.

⌐

Apart from the sea-area forecast, the two most impressive mantras of my childhood were the Litany of the Blessed Virgin at evening devotions and the Saturday afternoon results from the Football League. They helped to confer stability on a troubled world. You could count on them.

Queen of Angels, Queen of Patriarchs, Queen of Prophets, Queen of Apostles, Queen of Martyrs, Gate of Heaven, Morning Star, Cause of our Joy, Comforter of the Afflicted ...

Queen of the South, Leyton Orient, Plymouth Argyle, Brighton and Hove Albion, Nottingham Forest, Partick Thistle, Hamilton Academicals, Preston North End, Shrewsbury Town, Hartlepool United, Port Vale, Sheffield Wednesday ...

That was a strange name for a football team. Were there seven teams in Sheffield, one for every day of the week, and was Sheffield United a selection from the whole lot of them? Or maybe it was the other six days of the week put together, because the only teams ever mentioned were Sheffield United and Sheffield Wednesday? And what, then, was so special about Wednesday in Sheffield, that it could have a football team all to itself?

Soccer was a banned game. If you were caught playing it, even on the street, you would not be allowed to play hurling or Gaelic football ever again. But the lads from the Burma Road played soccer on the lane beside the Fair Green; they didn't care too much about the pronouncements of the GAA and other patriotic bodies. They were going to go to England as soon as they got the money, and being able to play soccer might be useful to them over there. Coming back from a game of hurling, we'd see them playing outside the garage at the entrance to the Fair Green, and pluck up the courage to shout a few mild taunts. Then we'd take to our heels down Main Street past the cinema, laughing at our own wit.

Are ye going to be playing for Sheffield Wednesday or Sheffield Thursday? Will ye be playing in Division Three North or Division Three South?

⤳

A mile was a long, long way to go.

'A mile?' said my mother. 'That'd be from old Mrs Bradley's house at the end of Green Terrace, out to the graveyard.'

Mrs Bradley's house was at the very end of the town; across the road from the last streetlight. If you walked out the road from there, you'd pass, first, the solicitor's house, second, my grandmother's house, third, after a while, the Horgans. After the Horgans, Smiley's Lane made a Y-fork with the road. It was called Smiley's Lane because Mr Smiley lived at the head of it. You walked on for a distance and you came to the house of Barbara's parents: the back yard of that house was where Barbara gave me the biggest hiding of my childhood, for getting cowdung on my Confirmation suit. Beating me with the flat of her hand across the face and head, punching me on the shoulders, she drove me from the porch of the farmhouse, across the farmyard, over a stile into a field. Then she stood menacingly over me while I tried to wipe off the stain with handfuls of wet grass. Why was she beating me so hard and so angrily, when she wasn't our housemaid any more and would soon be going to America?

My father used to bring us out to Barbara's parents' house on Sunday afternoons in winter and we went hunting rabbits with her brothers. Hunting was another thing that hardened us up, because we saw rabbits being attacked by dogs, and once we saw the dogs and Barbara's brothers, who carried big *bunawns* (sticks with knobs), doing a badger to death in a stream. We saw the badger's blood flowing with the water.

When we came back from the hunt, there was always a hot stew with dumplings in it, cooked by Barbara's mother. I loved those dumplings: it was the promise of them that kept my heart up during the long hunting treks in the cold.

Strangely, all the houses of the mile from Mrs Bradley's to the graveyard were on the left-hand side, across the road from the footpath. Except the Spirit House. That was a shed with whitewashed stone walls and a corrugated iron roof, and it was directly across the road from Barbara's parents' house. I once asked Daddy Corn, Barbara's grandfather, why the shed was called the Spirit House.

'Ah now,' he said, pulling on his chalk pipe, 'you're too young to be bothering with things like that.'

I thought it might have something to do with the spirits that Dominick said had come with the biscuits. The Spirit House might be the place where the man with the goats' milk got his Baby Power bottles: he drank the whiskey, then washed the bottle and put the goats' milk in for my grandmother, and made a cork with a rolled-up newspaper, because he was drunk and had lost the cap of the bottle. I was too young to be bothering about things like that because only adults drank whiskey.

The road continued on for another distance, and then it came to the graveyard. When I read *The Adventures of Tom Sawyer*, I visualized the episode of the cats following the ghosts and the warts following the cats as taking place in this hillocky, humpy graveyard where many of the graves were overgrown. James Colfer lived just across the road: his was the first real house on the right-hand side, but it didn't count, because it was at the very end of the mile. I imagined that if I was Tom Sawyer, I'd surely run for refuge to James Colfer when the commotion got going, because he was a friend of my grandmother's and rented her field – the one we were sent out to when my brothers and sister came to visit me on weekends.

~

Reading *The Adventures of Tom Sawyer* put me right about the world. In that book, adults and children seemed to lead parallel lives that never met even if they were extended forever. The ideal for children was to make their own lives as interesting as possible, independently of their parents.

From now on, I became more independent, not only inside my head, but outside it. There were a number of zones in my life which were almost entirely adult-free: fooling around with other altar boys after evening devotions in the friary; hurling and other activities on the Fair Green; going to the cinema and playing cowboy games afterwards; the world of reading and imagination; and the Republic of the Back Yard. When we were sent to play on the Fair Green, we were beginning to use it as a base for further explorations: venturing down the country roads, going into farmhouses and asking for drinks of water on hot summer days, meeting strange decrepit people in rural cottages, fording streams, picking nuts and berries, seeing what might happen. I was the leader of these expeditions. I had read about Tom Sawyer and was confident of adventures. But my world was still shadowy and below expectations: Christmas toys that broke on St Stephen's Day, adventures that never happened, races that were lost to youngsters half my size.

From now on, my mother sent me to get butter from the creamery for the shop. One or two of the others usually went with me. We walked down Main Street, turned left and walked to the very end of West Street, and there, just where the street gave way to hedges, was the creamery: steam rising from all kinds of silver-shining steel contraptions. I bought a dozen or eighteen pounds of butter. The wrapping paper of the butter was moist as I put the individual pounds one by one into my basket. Within a rectangle marked out on every semi-transparent wrapper, the name and address of the Co-operative and Dairy Society was printed, as well as the information that this was market butter. Market butter was different from country butter: it wasn't as strong, it had a lighter taste. My grandmother loved country butter, the kind farmers made at home, but I found it a bit sickening.

Going for butter was another activity that helped to toughen me, because a bully lived on West Street, just before the creamery. He'd usually pick on one of my younger brothers, and I'd have to stand up to him, put up my fists.

'All right so. Come on,' I'd say.

Like a lot of bullies, he was a coward underneath. He'd point to the younger brother he had just threatened.

'I'll fight *him*,' he'd volunteer, as if bullies were allowed that kind of choice and older brothers looked on, all part of the game.

'Why don't you fight someone your own size?' my younger brother would offer recklessly.

After a decent interval (but not too long, a matter of a few seconds) we'd walk away. Following such an en-counter, I always felt weak at the knees; my show of bravery had drained me.

Now I was hardly able to walk back up West Street, imagining the shadow behind me of the bully who had at last decided his honour was at stake and was going to thrash the living daylights out of me, *beat me into the middle of next week.* I got the strength of my legs back only when I turned right at the Cross and was in the familiar territory of Main Street.

And each day I was sent to the creamery, I had to be a little braver.

⤚

At about the age of ten, I began to take a serious interest in hurling, the game in which my county traditionally excelled, though the county just down the road (its border was another mile from the graveyard) nearly always beat us in the 1950s. The farmers of that county used to say to one another, 'We have the hay saved and soon we'll have the Cats bet.' *The Cats* was a nickname for my county's hurling team.

My father or my uncle brought me to an occasional game in the city. I was particularly fascinated by one of the county's corner forwards: he was a long stick-insect of a man with a cap pulled down over his eyes and his jersey pulled down over his shorts, so that you could hardly see the shorts, and the long vertically striped jersey made him look even taller than he was. Despite the cap pulled down over his eyes, he was very good at scoring points. It was a point when the ball went over the bar rather than under it into the net. But it took three balls going over the bar to equal one going under it; and so, for the sake of form, and even though he preferred scoring points from the corner of the field, the stick-insect with the long jersey occasionally weaved his way into the square and slammed the ball into the back of the net.

> Over the bar, says Lowry Meagher.
> Under it twice, says Michael Boyce.

Lowry Meagher was perhaps the most famous of the county's hurlers, but Michael Boyce was only a local news-agent who, as far as I knew, had never hurled in his life. I was intrigued that Lowry Meagher could score only one point in the verse, while the newsagent scored two goals, which was equal to six points. But Michael Boyce was a great 'hurler on the ditch'; he could tell you all the wrong things the team had done when they were beaten the previous Sunday. That was probably because he was a newsagent, and had read the Monday morning papers as soon as they were dropped off the bus.

When I began to play hurling, it had one thing in common with going hunting on winter afternoons: it helped to toughen me. But there was a big difference: I wanted to be a hurler. I loved hurling. I remember the first time I held in my hand a real *sliotar* or hurling ball. The stiff touch of it, the leathery smell of it, the joy and promise of it. The smell of the *sliotar* was a dream of scoring great goals and hearing the cheer of the crowd, which was a cheer for me alone, because I had slipped past the backs on a solo-run, tapping the ball up and down on the end of my stick, slamming it past the gaping goalkeeper. The hurling balls that children played with weren't real *sliotars:* they got soggy in the wet, the stitching came easily undone, they were soft and inert, they turned grey instead of staying white, and above all they didn't have 'O'Neill' printed on them. To touch my first real hurling ball was, for the moment, as good as winning an All-Ireland medal. The whole career of a famous hurler was implicit in the feel and the smell and the glossy new whiteness of it.

It wasn't that easy, however, to become a hurler. First you had to have a proper hurling stick or *camán*, made of ash; not the kind of child's one you could buy in Kelly's or Fenwick's, made of synthetic sawdust, that broke in two if you looked crooked at it.

There was a man living in Green Terrace who made proper hurleys. He'd make a hurley for you if you brought him a plank of ash. My mother made some enquiries among her customers, and one of them, a spare-time carpenter, brought a plank of ash into town strapped to the crossbar of his bike. We had to be careful not to call him by his nickname, 'Red', because he hated it, and if any one of us said, 'Here's Red with the timber for the hurley', he'd strap the plank back on his bike and cycle home and we'd probably never see him again.

Unfortunately, the hurley-maker on Green Terrace had a one-track mind. He specialized in senior hurleys, and it didn't matter what age or size you were when you came to him and asked 'Will you make me a hurley?' He'd hardly look at you, simply take the plank and produce after a few weeks a *camán* that was the right size for the corner forward of the county team, but for you at the age of ten it was totally inappropriate; when you gripped the top with both hands and tried your first swing, you could hardly get the *bos* or blade, the part which was supposed to make contact with the ball, off the ground. Your wrists began to ache with the effort of swinging it.

But I was very attached to this hurley that hadn't changed much from its former state of being a plank, because it was my first *real* one, made of ash. I was proud of it, despite the fact that when I stood it up against my side, it went far beyond the top of my hip and almost reached my chest.

A suitable hurley would only reach as far as your hip when you stood it up against your side. Similarly, you knew a bicycle was suitable if you could lean over its crossbar and touch the centre of the pedal-disc. When I stayed with my maternal grandmother, I learned to cycle on a 'High Nellie', a bicycle so tall that my hand over the crossbar couldn't even reach the topmost pedal, never mind the centre of the disc. After several falls, I learned the trick of pedalling without putting a leg over the crossbar: I cycled standing, my body at an angle to the vertical of the bike, like a sail leaning in a cross-wind. Now I was learning to play hurling with a High Nellie of a hurling stick.

⌒

I don't remember crying much as a child. Given the kind of childhood I had, it would have been better if I had cried a lot. But I didn't, and that is probably why I was in such a tearful state a few years ago, writing the first draft of this memoir.

Apart from the day I told my father I wanted to be a priest, and the evening my grandmother beat me with a switch, I can remember only one other occasion when I cried outright. It was the Sunday of the All-Ireland hurling final between Cork, my father's county, and my own county, my mother's county. We were all in the parlour listening to Micheál Ó hEithir's commentary on the radio. The other children sided with Cork, probably out of fear, or to ingratiate themselves with my father. I was passionately identified with my own county's hurlers. My mother sided with them too, but in a detached, diplomatic sort of way. Fortunes swayed, until eventually Cork scored a goal or point that put them in the lead with only a minute or so left to play. When the final whistle blew, my father crowed with delight, teasing me triumphantly, and the others joined abjectly in what I saw as derision. I burst into tears. The world was against me and what I stood for. I was being punished for having a mind of my own.

(*I'm hearing you, Ciaran,* mocks the ghost.)

My father rounded on me. 'Take your beating like a man, or what in all this goodness gracious is wrong with you? Do you want to be a sissy all your life?'

'What's wrong with ye for God's sake?' my mother implored. 'Sure it's only a game.'

(*I'm taking that on board, Ciaran. I hear where you're coming from. Have a nice weekend. And keep taking the tablets.*)

↶

I was going to be a great hurler when I grew up. I'd play for my county, my mother's county, and we'd beat Cork every time, and that would cause my father *a damned sight of trouble.* I'd never raise my voice to him again, I'd say nothing, just hover round the corner of the field with my cap pulled down over my eyes so that he'd think I couldn't even see the ball, but when it was sent into the square, I'd appear out of nowhere and double on it with a clean overhead stroke.

The backs and the goalie look around bewildered: the ball has disappeared. But they know from the cheer of the crowd, from the green flag raised by the umpire, that it's gone into the net. I look up to where my father is sitting among the crowd, the Hurler on the Ditch, the Giver of Advice, but this isn't the kind of look that invites praise, because wanting praise from him is a waste of time. No; it is a look of defiance.

There you are now, that's the winning goal against your county, scored at the last minute just to make it all the more bitter for you.

But it wasn't that easy to become a great hurler, especially when you had to play with a half-plank. In the first match I played on the Fair Green, I hardly once made contact with the ball. The stick was so cumbersome, I was like a slow-motion action replay in the middle of live footage.

'Ah for God's sake,' said my mother when I came home with my story of disappointment, 'how could he hurl with that yoke?'

She sent me up to Green Terrace to get the hurley-maker to pare down my hurley. He wasn't pleased with the implicit criticism of his craft, but agreed to have a look at the stick when he got the time. A half-plank, however, returned as three-sevenths of a plank, and my difficulties continued.

But I persisted, borrowing lighter hurleys whenever I could, even picking up ones which had been tossed aside during games because a section of the *bos* had broken off.

Learning the craft with inadequate implements, by the time I went to boarding school with the first really suitable hurley in my luggage, I was already quite skilful and found a place on the junior team. But the boarding school was in Munster, and Father Nessan, a fervent advocate of 'ground hurling', tried to wean me from my own county's style of always lifting the ball into the hand. Ground hurling might have been more effective, but it didn't give me much of a chance to show off. The Cats were too fancy, Father Nessan said. That's why they couldn't beat Cork or Tipperary: they wasted too much time trying to get the ball into their hands. In the boarding school, I was nicknamed the Pushkin.

9

Rites and teens

The sea at Spanish Point is calm today, hardly a wave. The broad sweep of it from one end of the bay to the other and outwards to the horizon is glass-like except for the flounce at my feet. This great expanse of sea and shore jars with my sense of con- strictedness, the feeling that my head is a narrow little time-capsule where I am ensconced with the flotsam of childhood memories. But these fragments are precious all the same; they are the salvage of storms on another sea.

Today the sea is not suitable for my wave-therapy. The calm breadth of it puts broader vistas in mind, signals the impossibility of staying in my memoir-hut, the cabin of my final draft (a mobile home in a nearby caravan park) among the relics of my early years.

And so, my straitened Irish childhood, my old Polonius behind the arras: *to draw toward an end with you ...*

⌐

The various rites of passage that occur to a child around the ages of eleven and twelve are not particularly interesting in my case, because my shadow was the one going through them. Most of the time, I was in the Elsewhere with the ghost of my father's son.

Sometimes we searched for sanctifying grace in the Elsewhere, but it was inaccessible. Totally invisible and un-measurable, like the ether which preceded Einstein's theory of light, sanctifying grace was perhaps the hallmark of 1950s' Ireland: a parallel universe where things were completely different from what they were in reality, but which made no difference to the way reality was ordered. The solicitor's soul could be without sanctifying grace, while Moll Bailey's could be brimming with it; but the solicitor would stay the solicitor and Moll Bailey would always be Fleaballs. You could be very unhappy and have a soul full of sanctifying grace, and be very happy and have none at all, like the happy pagans. The sacraments were supposed to be *outward signs of inward grace*, but there was an enormous uncrossable chasm between the sign and the substance.

The machine of my body is usually driven by my shadow, but the ghost sometimes takes over the wheel. I have a recurrent dream of being in a rust-eaten Fiat 128 (the only car I have ever owned) which is careering out of control down a steep hill of multiple hairpin bends. That is my ghost in the machine. My shadow, however, is an excessively careful driver, the kind that gets on everyone's nerves, who pulls out in front of you on a country road at ten miles an hour and proceeds at the same speed, causing a tailback.

My shadow is fearful of life, passive, accepting, eager to

please, conformist, anxious, self-absorbed, timid, shy, retentive, depressed and generally lacking in energy. But despite all this, it has an enormous power over me: the grip of inertia. From the time when the atom of love was split by my father's careless words, inertia has dominated the here-and-now of my existence, and the energy of my personality has been trapped in the Elsewhere, escaping occasionally in various manifestations, such as the raver at the window of memory or the curser of waves or the boy who says *Ah, scutter!* at the breakfast table of his polite uncle and aunt.

⌒

My Confirmation Test: A few months before my oral examination in Christian Doctrine took place, my father had changed schools into a different diocese, and there was a new catechism to be learned by heart, the answers longer than those in my old catechism, though in slightly more accessible English. When the bishop arrived at the school to examine us, my shadow wouldn't dare give him the old answers it knew, and it couldn't remember the new formulae. (My ghost, however, could come in from the street and recite, word-perfect, verse upon verse of doggerel.)

The bishop asked me, 'What is a sacrament?'

'A sacrament is … a sacrament is … Baptism is a sacrament.'

'He doesn't seem to understand the question,' the bishop said to my father.

'Well, that's extraordinary,' my father replied. 'It's not like him at all. Maybe he's not well today.'

156

Rather enlightened for his time, the bishop then asked me to explain a sacrament in my own way. Using the words of my old catechism, I said a sacrament was an outward sign of inward grace. The bishop was satisfied.

'I don't know what in all this goodness gracious is wrong with you, and why you couldn't answer first as last,' my father said to me afterwards. 'You seem to be going around in a dream most of the time.'

I knew a lot of things in theory but couldn't answer them in practice, because when I was in the Elsewhere, my shadow was stupid.

⤸

The Primary Certificate Examination, Mental Arithmetic Paper: half an hour to do twenty sums. Trying desperately to come out of the Elsewhere, that region of my mind where I usually lived, which was difficult to leave, a mathematics-free zone, a country alien to quantity, precision, exactitude and what happens to be the case. Begging for an exit visa which would allow me to be at this desk, doing these sums, for this important examination. For thirty minutes.

If a man bought a cow for £3-12s-6d and sold it for four guineas, how much profit did he make? Multiply $3\frac{1}{2}$ by $4\frac{3}{4}$. You must do it all in your mind, write down only the answer. Or you can (if you must) work it out on your sheet of roughwork paper beforehand.

A large drop of ink formed on the tip of my poised nib and as I moved the pen towards the sheet, to write in my answer to Question 16, the ink fell on the answer to

Question 9, forming a blob that also partly obscured the answer to Question 10. But there was no time left for repeating these questions; I still had four to do, and there were only two minutes left.

I put the uncompleted, still-wet answer sheet into the envelope provided and worried for months that I would fail. I passed, but my father couldn't understand why my performance had been so mediocre.

'I suppose you were in a dream half the time,' he said.

No, no. I was in the Elsewhere, because you made mathematics a nightmare.

⮌

Confirmation Day: After the church service, I walk proudly down Main Street in my new suit. There is a red rosette, with my Confirmation medal as its centrepiece, pinned to the lapel of my coat. I have attained the status of true and perfect Christian. I also have long trousers, like Michael Rodgers.

The music teacher is walking up the street on the other side.

'Oh breeches, where did you get the chap?' he calls out.

That's the end of the groping for you, ya fucker, says my ghost, forty-five years too late.

⮌

There's no such thing as Santa Claus: At the beginning of my first Christmas holidays from boarding school, my father drove to collect me. As was usual when he wanted to have a heart-to-heart talk with me, a few miles from home he parked the car on the side of the road. I had just turned thirteen.

'I suppose you know by now ... ,' he began.

And indeed I did. But it wasn't because anyone had told me in so many words. My belief in Santa Claus seemed to have fallen gradually from me, the way leaves fall unnoticed from a tree until one day you look out and the branches are bare.

My father gave me a long lecture on the meaning of Santa Claus, but I wasn't really listening.

⌒

I get to play Santa Claus: My father spent the following Christmas in hospital. At the time he was reported to have a non-malignant tumour in one lung. I learned only much later that he had cancer and was very sick indeed, not far from death. But he survived for another forty years with, as he put it, 'a lung and a quarter'. My father had a fierce hold on the fundamental matter of continuing to live. Perhaps life itself was his greatest treasure, greater than his ambitions and dreams.

In any case, his hospitalization during my second Christmas home from boarding school meant that I became Santa Claus. On Christmas Eve, my mother gave me twenty pounds and I boarded the bus to go to the city in search of presents. When I returned at six or seven in the evening, and got off the bus carrying two large bags, my brothers and sister were all waiting. *What did you get for me?*

What did you get for me? they chorused. Angry and embarrassed, I denied that there was anything, for any of them, in those bulging bags; nothing but stuff for the shop, which my mother had sent me to get because the vans from the city didn't travel around Christmas, and she would be opening the shop again on St Stephen's Day. *And so on and so forth …*

It was long-winded, convoluted, demanded mental agility, the ability to think on the hoof; barely plausible, it was accepted with relief, like all the resolutions of Santa Claus's contradictions which parents are called on to invent. (It was not my shadow who was speaking on this occasion.)

↩

The Theory of the Sneezing Ghost: On reflection, I have to admit that fairly substantial transfers of energy from the ghost in the Elsewhere to the here-and-now of my bodily existence must have occurred throughout my life (not just small doses every now and then); otherwise I would have died long ago of the shadow's stranglehold. Could it be that, time and time again, various irritations have caused the ghost to sneeze? Could it be that ghost-energy (divisible, as the soul is in certain ancient theories) has escaped in varying quantities from the Elsewhere in those sneezes and entered my life-as-it-is, recharging my dead batteries?

My new therapist's buzz-phrases have been setting my teeth on edge. Despite the real help he has been to me (among other things, my relations with shop assistants have improved), there are times when I want to hit him.

160

These are the times when he uses more buzz-phrases than usual. We meet early in the morning, and sometimes perhaps he's tired after a night on the tiles (therapists are human too), and the barrage of psychobabble is a screen behind which he is collecting his thoughts. This consideration, however, does little to assuage the grating effect on my nerves of a continuous stream of therapyspeak. I have had to devise a coping strategy.

My therapist is a witch-doctor. I have hired him to get my ghost to sneeze energy into me, and break the stranglehold of my shadow. This demands that we meet every week and talk for an hour. No more, no less: he is very strict about that; the hour is a magic circle which we must enter once a week. He calls his remedy 'the talking cure', but the conversation part is merely to lull the ghost into a false sense of security. It is important not to mention the ghost, of course; we are to speak about the shadow, and the anima, the mother and the cave and the trickster, and all the other Jungian archetypes (except the spirit, which sounds too like the ghost). But the most important part of the talking cure is the witch-doctor's copious use, throughout the conversations, of the magic formulae: *I can take that on board, I can relate to that (in a meaningful way), I'm hearing you, I hear what you're saying, I hear where you're coming from,* and so on. A given combination of these formulae will cause any ghost to sneeze, but in the case of a particular ghost, that combination is unknown and has to be discovered.

I need the witch-doctor badly now, because my ghost hasn't sneezed (in a meaningful way) for five years. That is why I must not only put up with, but be glad of, the magic formulae, the crucial part of the talking cure.

⤺

The ghost sneezes me a teenage rebellion: For the first two years my shadow thrived in that boarding school in Munster, on the borrowed energy of a rigorous institutional regime, where everything was predictable and controlled, where I knew for certain what earned approval and what deserved punishment. Back at home, I had never known what to do to please my father or Barbara. There were no clearly defined guidelines: I only knew what the rule was at the moment of punishment. My father said *If you do that again, I'll beat you into the middle of next week,* and when I did it again, he was in better humour and didn't beat me; but then, suddenly, in the middle of the next week, he beat me for something else, a previously unheard-of transgression.

My shadow is fear of punishment and the desire to please, and it thrived in an environment where there were very clear directions on how it could ingratiate itself. In that rigorous boarding-school environment, my shadow even developed an intelligence.

And so, for two years, I was a model student. Then something caused my ghost to sneeze mightily. Perhaps it was the rush of adolescent hormones.

⤺

The new person that came to light in boarding school, an indeterminate mixture of ghost and shadow, was a pleasantly cynical adolescent, hardened by participation in sport, confident of his academic prowess. Stubborn, even rebellious, but having an academic record the authorities did not deny, he became an admired figure, a sort of natural leader among the boys. The authorities, too, admired him despite his bolshie proclivities, but inexplicably – even to himself – he refused their offer of a prefectship. He preferred the charisma of unofficial leadership in low-profile anti-authoritarian exploits such as ducking the communal walks, smoking, organizing poker schools in the dormitories on wet days during mid-afternoon recreation, playing the piano with his toes as he roared out the words of *Jailhouse Rock*. In class, he openly defied teachers with harsh condemning tongues, and as a result often found himself in the Rector's office, where he was admonished to think of the sacrifices his parents were making to send him to the college. 'You're stubborn,' the Rector would say to him, 'but you have character.' Or vice versa.

He had a bad-tempered maths-teacher, one who no doubt reminded him of the dead child's father; and that, perhaps, was why he narrowly failed to get an Intermediate Certificate scholarship, losing a few vital marks in a surprisingly below-par performance in arithmetic and algebra. (In art, he got honours, despite answering only the questions that the teacher hadn't covered during the year.)

This new person had an attractive personality (for an adolescent). His nihilism was witty and charming. Something of an aesthete, he read extra-curricular works such as

The Picture of Dorian Gray and *Boswell's Life of Johnson*. Between papers at the Intermediate Certificate examinations, while others were feverishly swotting their notes, he sat on the steps leading up to the Top Plot, reading *Dracula*.

He was physically attractive to some of the senior boys. One day on the sports field, while they were sitting around waiting for some game or other to begin, a senior boy began to fondle him, pretending it was just a demonstration of what to do when you went to the pictures with a girl. But he wouldn't let the senior touch his private parts.

He was more interested in girls, but there weren't any in his life. It was forbidden to associate with them, not that the boarders ever met them, except perhaps on one of the very infrequent 'free days' when they were let loose around the streets of Cork. Even then, there was the danger that a solid citizen, recognizing where a boy came from by his blazer, would report him to the college for having been seen with a girl. That was why, one free day, he and a few other boys smuggled out ordinary clothes, and changed in the bus-station toilet as soon as they got off the bus. He met a girl that afternoon, and took her to a café for lemonade and buns, but when he asked her to come to the pictures, she said she had to go somewhere else.

He wanted to go to a dance, but he had to be back in the college too early for that. Dancing was considered an occasion of sin by the college authorities, since the proximity to a female body which it contrived could lead to an erection and subsequent bad thoughts, inadmissible for boys supposed to be nurturing vocations to the priesthood.

He was more interested in girls, but he didn't know

what to say to them. Sometimes he masturbated in the dark of the dormitory, covering his penis with a handkerchief in case the Dean would see traces of sperm on the sheets the next morning. Sometimes he touched himself and imagined he was touching a girl.

His summer holidays were a hell of dawning sexuality. He would sit in the café where the teenagers met to play the town's only jukebox, and wear a wide grin. Afraid to smile because one of his front teeth was bad and another had been chipped in a hurling match, he would sit in the café and be infatuated by a girl to whom he didn't know what to say.

But one day down by the river, in the long hot summer of 1959, when he was fifteen, he talked with two girls from the Burma Road. The two girls, Helen and Teresa, were wearing bathing suits. Teresa had bad teeth, so he talked more with Helen. After a while, he kissed her; it seemed the thing to do. She kissed him back, and they kissed on for about ten minutes or so. Then the girls had to go home.

So that was the way things happened with girls! The secret seemed to be that you talked to them in an ordinary way, about this and that, just as if you hadn't the remotest hint of an erection; and then, after a while, you kissed them, and if they wanted to, they kissed you back. There wasn't any mystery about it; all that time he had spent trying to solve the enigma had been wasted anguish.

It was pure exhilaration to walk back home along the river path after this significant life-event, the pleasure of it still on his mouth. To take the chance and get away with it; not only to get away with it, but to meet a willing response. To kiss and be kissed. It wasn't true love, of course, or even falling in love. But in one sense it was greater than those, something without which they could not occur. It was the discovery that he was eligible.

He wasn't supposed to do it, of course, especially not with girls from the Burma Road; above all not with girls from the Burma Road who were wearing only their bathing suits. But somehow, at the time, it seemed natural and right. It was only later, when his father was waiting on the pavement outside the shop, shouting down the street in Irish, *A Chiaráin tar anseo, Ciaran come here*, and interrogated him about why he was spending so much time down by the river, that it began to feel wrong.

But the memory of those first kisses was too strong; stronger than his guilt, stronger than his father. He wanted more, although he knew it wasn't right. He had a vocation to be a priest, but he wanted a girl. That was the year he became one of the lads who went with girls to the back row of the cinema or down the lane behind the parish church.

But down by the river was *the* place to be that long hot summer. Even when he wasn't talking *to* the girls, he could talk *about* them; he and his mates would sit in a circle on the bank, 'studying form' and passing remarks. Every riverside afternoon brought him further away from his father, and his father, sensing this increasing distance, was always on the look-out for his return, ready with admonitions.

His returns grew later and later as the heatwave entrenched itself, expanding time. Young emigrants, returned for holidays from England, began to appear beside the river and join his group, freely distributing strange cigarettes: Camel, RN, Senior Service. The jokes they told were superior to the local ones; in essence as salacious as those doing the rounds in the town, they had an exoticism of foreign customs and settings that lent them novelty and sophistication. The high point of that riverside epoch was a marathon joke-telling session which involved about twenty participants. It happened at the zenith of summer, just before the heat could no longer endure itself. One joke from that session impressed him above all the others, almost as if he dimly perceived in it a crude metaphor of his own situation.

There was this guy driving a busload of priests and nuns through the desert and he was bursting for a piss. He was too embarrassed to get out and do it, because there was nothing to hide behind. This went on for hours, until at last he saw a jeep driving in the opposite direction. So he gets out and waves down the jeep and asks the chap driving it, 'Ere, mate, will you do me a favour? Sure, says the other. And the busdriver says, I want you to go into the next town and get me twelve white horses and twelve black horses. And I want you to put twelve white saddles on the twelve black horses, and twelve black saddles on the twelve white horses. Have you got that? I think so, mate, says the driver of the jeep. I'll go over it just to make sure. You want me to go into the next town and get you twelve white horses and twelve black horses. And you want me to put twelve white saddles on the twelve black horses and twelve black saddles on the... 'Ere, mate! Are you pissing down my leg?

Then one day in the new school term, sitting in Greek class, at his brown desk scored with the names and dates of previous occupants, he suddenly feels that he is a hundred years old, that he has been around since the beginning of time, that he has seen too much and it is time for him to die. *Apothanein thelo.* But like the Sybil's, his boredom is immortal.

In his first senior year, he comes within a hair's breadth of expulsion for being in possession of a detective novel with a naked woman on the cover. At the start of the third term, at the railway station before boarding the bus for the college, he sends a postcard to a girl in his home town: *Hi Betty. Hope you're not in as bad a humour as I am today.* Then he worries that if Betty writes back to him, even if she sends a letter, in a sealed envelope, the Rector will see it, because the boys' incoming mail is regularly inspected. Her letter is given to him unopened, but there is nothing in it only local chat.

In his final senior term, he is once more in trouble: there has been a raid on the students' lockers and, in his, an issue of *World Digest* has been discovered, one which contains an article entitled 'Amateur Night at the Striptease'. Again he is summoned to the office, but the Rector takes a long-term view of the materially grave situation, seeing that he is about to leave the college, in the normal course of events, for good.

'Whatever happened to you?' the Rector remonstrates. 'When you came here first, you had the makings of a great saint of our Order. We were so proud of you. And now look at what you are reading….'

The Rector drops the depraved periodical into his litter bin and dismisses my vicious alter ego.

⌐

A few weeks ago, I had a waking dream: I am alone in a barren landscape and a shining cloud appears above me. The light from the cloud intensifies, descending in a wide shaft that becomes a long luminous stairway, beginning just a few feet in front of me. And a voice I know too well comes from the cloud: *A Chiaráin, tar anseo, Ciaran, Ciaran, come into the light.* Stung with rage, I jump up in the bed and shout: FUCK OFF, DAD! LEAVE ME ALONE!

Today I told my therapist about it, and he actually laughed. He is a bit on the plump side, and he laughed so heartily, I could see his belly shaking.

'I hear where you're coming from, Ciaran,' he said, regaining his posture.

10

One sweet note

As a teenager, you were a fine lad; insouciant, not caring much for anybody, you were yourself, and harmlessly you used to rib that other brainbox in your class, the one who was nicknamed the Critic. *Whoo-hoo the Critic! Whoo-hoo the Critic!* you used to taunt when he looked at your latest poem and damned it with faint praise: *Rather good. Reminiscent of Dryden, of course.*

Whoo-hoo the Critic! because some kind of courage had been born within you and you didn't care what he or anybody else said about you. You were yourself and yet you moved among them all as a fish in water.

Your voice was you: it could be heard in a continuous monologue on the playing field, a commentary on everything, a rolling stream of dry unappreciated jokes, but all it really said was *This is me; I am and I am I*, a seabird doing a loop above the waves.

But back home your mother said *Ciaran, you have a terrible temper*, as if it had dropped into you out of the sky, yet the truth is you showed remarkable restraint: you were still in awe of him and perhaps you didn't want to desecrate again that already desecrated bond. Sometimes you burnt sullen in his presence and paradoxically you found release from it all in the confinement of a boarding school: at least there they thought you were somehow precious, a great makings of what they wanted you to be, and they watched you come and go; they kept their eyes on you, as your father did in old age when you visited, his gaze following you nervously around the room. But you were a fine lad and had that insouciant thing in you.

⌒

I would have done anything for your love but you stood divided up at the schoolhouse door, a cubist assemblage of your own fragments, a *Guernica* contradicting the natural forms and deep hues of autumn. Only one fragment of many would receive me, but I proved too big for it, a small boy wanting to be loved by his father was too big for that shard of your attention, and you ejected me as the eye ejects a mote of dust.

I would have done anything for your love:

> For the error bred in the bone
> Of each woman and each man
> Craves what it cannot have,
> Not universal love
> But to be loved alone.

Maybe I would have been satisfied with a little less. Not to be loved alone, just to be loved. Just to *know* that you loved me – unconditionally. But I was never sure with you, from one minute to the next.

And maybe that heedless teenager I became should have done time for you, battered you to within an inch of your life, and you'd have changed your tune and a prodigal father would have wept and embraced his child as in some hackneyed Hollywood scenario. But you burnt on inside and so did I, two sullen old fires filling the space between them with smoke.

And maybe the two of us should have shouted *Whoo-hoo the Critic! Whoo-hoo the Critic!* lifting our voices in derision, and the smoke would have cleared into a motionless autumn morning where father and son could walk and talk together. But instead you as regards me and I as regards you became a silence, the dart of fear in your eyes as well as mine whenever I met you in your mellowed old age. And what is silence because no one knows what it is or what's hidden in it and they have to invent hostile yarns to fill the vacuum? And the truth is that neither of us knew how to bring what was hidden into the open, no more than you knew in your last illness what to do with your demented hands.

Why is the sky blue? Why is the grass green? Why are the children running wildly among the falling leaves? Are they running like that because they know that they are loved?

And maybe I too will be loved if I run with them, because my father the Master is watching from the school door.

172

I will run the wildest because my father is watching. I will be the best runner among falling leaves.

⤺

What I particularly like about my nine-year-old son is the sense of irrepressible life he conveys. To be precise, my ghost is the one who likes that buoyancy, that bubbling energy. Already my ghost is third generation, indulgent like Granny-in-Cork or, irony of ironies, like my father in my son's memory, *a kind old man who loved me.* My shadow, however, is irritated by unpredictable outbursts of childish high spirits.

This morning at breakfast, my son is, as usual, plying me with his infinite demands. He needs a new string for his guitar, he needs a skateboard because skateboarding is the fashion among his friends this summer (last year it was rollerblading); he needs a new sister or brother (why can't you and Mammy just go upstairs and make one?). He needs, he needs, he needs....

His Playstation has broken down, and he reminds me that I promised to get it fixed. I say I'll definitely get someone to mend it today, if I can, and he's satisfied for the time being.

Suddenly he looks up from his cornflakes and says: 'In a real world, everything would work properly, wouldn't it, Dad?'

'I suppose so,' I reply, wondering if I have another Platonist to contend with.

Is there a real world to match the quietness, the silence, the non-existence, of my father's final years? A world where one sweet note is sounded on a string and is enough because it resonates forever? Where the place I grew up in is transposed into its mute music?

Pocketing my list of things to do in town, I walk out to a perfect morning: autumnal, pure surface.